Get Governed - Buildi
Governance

Build a Data Governance program the business can understand and IT will support.

You work with information every day. You're an expert. It's why your boss asked you to implement a Data Governance program for your company. Even though you have worked places where you were held to certain governance standards, you haven't ever had to set up a program before. Where do you start? What does it mean to be a well governed organization? How do you get buy-in from the business and not step outside of the guard rails established by the Information Technology group?

Morgan Templar has been in your shoes. With over twenty years of experience serving as a bridge between business and technology, she knows what is important to both sides of the house. Templar will help you:

- Understand what can be accomplished with little or no financial investment.
- Find the keys to ensure alignment with both business and IT stakeholders.
- Set up success criteria and prove that *You Rocked This*!
- Develop the right roles and responsibilities for your company's program.
- Navigate the transition from set-up to ongoing operations.

With the same mix of fact and passion as "The 4 Disciplines of Execution: Achieving your wildly important goals" by Sean Covey, Chris McChesney, and Jim Huling, "The Innovators Dilemma," by Clayton Christensen, and "Traction: Get a grip on your business," by Gino Wickman, Templar takes a topic perceived as dry and quickly carries you to the, "So What" of Data Governance – why it matters and how it benefits your organization. No other book on Data Governance provides such a clear roadmap to success while keeping you awake and entertained with stories of how Data Governance has made a difference in the lives of customers and employees. With millions of data points changing every day, there is no time to waste! Time to Get Governed!

Get Governed

Building World Class Data Governance Programs

By Morgan Templar

Ivory Lady Publishing
Rescue, California

Copyright

Advance Praise

"Healthcare organizations are just starting to realize the potential value of the data that they are sitting on, and 'Get Governed' explains both the "why" and the "how" to help organizations find the hidden value of those data assets. Whether you're just getting started, or have been in information management for years, 'Get Governed' provides a practical, down-to-earth guide to get your organization on the right path to effective data governance."

– Glen Schuster, Founder and Principal, Skrymir Data Strategies.
Featured in "Why Big Data is a Big Deal" – Modern Healthcare Executive. Former Chief Technology Officer, Centene Corporation

"Healthcare has seen an incredible amount of investment internally and externally related to Data, Analytics and Informatics, but if you objectively review how successful these investments have been, you will see that success has not been because of the technology and innovation but rather because of the effectiveness of governance. This book provides a unique perspective on the missing link in many organizations' Data Strategies – Governance. Governance is not just about control and decision making, it's how you enable the effective use of Data and Information to drive value and align it to the stakeholders which companies serve. Growth in healthcare company's data consumption and processing continues to grow exponentially, however across the board most companies struggle with driving the value they expect to receive from this volume and investment; putting in place the right decision making and governance processes at the enterprise level is critical. 'Get Governed' helps put some context and structure around these efforts."

– Bill Fandrich, Senior Vice President and Chief Information Officer, Blue Cross and Blue Shield of Michigan

"This book is long overdue. Having worked in healthcare for the past three decades, it's clear we simply didn't know what we didn't know. 'Get Governed' is an excellent how-to guide that will help any healthcare organization simplify, standardize and get smarter about managing their data. Once you "Get Governed" lean in and "Govern with Gusto" to exploit data differentiation with your providers, members and stakeholders to drive a real competitive advantage...perhaps the "Get Governed" sequel."

– Nanci Ziegler, Vice President Customer Experience,
McKesson Health Services/Change Healthcare

Dedication

For Stephen

Forever, my love!

Table of Contents

Get Governed

Building World Class Data Governance Programs

Foreword

Not all topics present an instant allure, get us to pay attention, to care, to get involved. Data is a topic that can cause eyes to glaze over, but the governance of data is the process of deciding which data we truly need and why, something we should all care about. Because data has quietly and quickly reached a critical mass of volume and complexity, the immense opportunities we seek with it can only be achieved when matched with a process of refining it to the few elements among the many that deserve the title "asset." However, without the attention, understanding and involvement of every person within organizations, with roles large and small, data governance process cannot unfold. That is precisely why we need Morgan Templar sharing her practical experiences on this little known but highly important topic about data.

Passionate people like Morgan can change the way we all look at our surroundings, how we approach problems as well as opportunities. In this case, Morgan is sharing how data presents endless opportunities once the right structure, leadership, conversations and cultural shift begin to take place. Whether you picked up this book for curiosity or because you are now responsible for delivering Data Governance to an organization, "Get Governed" is a well-composed guide that will change the way you think about the problem. Morgan thoughtfully lays out the reasons for Data Governance, the setup, the buy-in, the proof-points and the successes and failures to learn from. Morgan takes you on this journey in such an approachable manner that average people and experienced data management professionals alike can all reap the benefits of her experience and knowledge.

Morgan's experience and insight is what makes this book worth reading. She has been involved in Data Governance long before there was a title to the subject. And she committed to solving these problems long before we knew it would be considered critical for competitive advantage in digital enterprises. Morgan did not set out on a career in data governance. Instead she approached her roles as a problem solver at the nexus between systems, people and data. Her experiences from careers in financial services and healthcare are insightful and relatable to all. It is unique to find people who know both the business challenges and the systems needed to support these challenges, but Morgan possesses that über quality of commanding an ability to communicate on the topic.

So why data governance? Phrases of the day are "Data is the New Oil" or "Data is Gold" because data has become a very pervasive resource. Yet it has no use or utility without a means for refining it to the important parts. Data Governance is the means for an organization to refine the many data attributes collected, stored and flowing through the enterprise into a common understanding of the few that matter and how to treat them. Data Governance can be broken down into driving value for three core objectives: Analytics and Insights, Operational Excellence and Compliance & Reporting. Use cases related to each define a reason for why data must be trusted and the means for how it must be governed to deliver trust.

Done well, Data Governance delivers your ability to trust the outcomes of your analytics, to operationalize programs that will improve efficiency, and it is knowing you can trust you are doing what is needed to stay compliant. If you believe in a future of automation then you must believe in the need for data governance. Even a future with artificial intelligence depends on a trusted data set and a trusted algorithm. We will not reach a meaningful outcome of automation unless we can trust the data driving the patterns used to model the automation.

We live within extreme complexity and a need to simplify. Organizations find it hard to connect the dots between layers of data usage on the business side and systems supporting them on the technology side. Understanding what business parameters are most critical for the enterprise is imperative in understanding how best to utilize a technology landscape for execution on the desired business outcomes. Today we look to a digital transformation agenda to deliver simplicity for the end user or customer, and data is at the heart of our challenge.

Digital Transformation is a shift in technology and a shift in culture to understand data as the work product for creation and consumption in a new ecosystem. New businesses are formed purely on the use of data as a key tenant of their business model, however more traditional "bricks and mortar" businesses are recognizing the need for digital transformation to present greater agility. This next era of business is only going to be successful by embracing data governance and the importance of the trusted insight you will gain.

You are well-equipped to "Get Governed" with Morgan Templar as your coach. Enjoy the journey!

Marie Klok Crump
Chief Operating Officer
DATUM LLC
September 7, 2017
Annapolis, MD

Introduction

Go to any business conference these days and chances are at least one of the speakers will be talking about Data Governance in one form or another. Don't believe me? Look at the speaker line-up. She is speaking about Data Quality. He is speaking about implementing a project. They are covering their comprehensive method of validating information. Someone else will cover their document management system and how it has allowed them to transition to a "paperless" business model. There will be at least one presentation about business process management or process improvement.

What do these topics have in common? They are all aspects of Data Governance. The most common topic, which is the first component of data governance, is Information Management. They are similar; Information Management is a subset of Data Governance. Data governance takes management of information to the next level by including systems management, data quality, policy management, business rules, business process management and workflows, and much more.

You may be thinking that this isn't relevant to you. Your business is too small to worry about all this structure. Or maybe you are already part of a large corporation that has many of the things listed above. In both cases, you will find that the benefits of getting data governance right are available regardless of the size of your enterprise. And getting right with your data is critical to your company's survival in the 21st Century.

Chapter 1 – Why Governance Matters

"There is no such thing as JUST DATA.
In a world full of billions of pieces of data, we must
remember that each one is critical for someone.
Data can be Life or Death."
Morgan Templar

Mark was a Ranger in the US Army and an Iraq War veteran. He has been exposed to some very unusual chemicals and environmental toxins. While he has mostly recovered, and lives a pretty normal life, he is highly allergic to many medications and everyday chemicals, such as organic counter cleaners. As a result, he often goes into full-on Anaphylactic shock. One of the treatments often administered in the Emergency Room, following his self-administered epinephrine doses, is dopamine. Unfortunately for Mark, dopamine is one of the medications he is highly allergic to.

After a recent exposure to something (sometimes hard to identify the exact allergen), he was rushed to the hospital. When he arrived at the Emergency Room (ER) via ambulance, his wife, Jenny, was five minutes behind them in the car racing from work to the hospital. Mark is at this ER often. His medical records are in their system, including his medication allergies. The first thing they do, of course, is to put in an IV. Mark is barely conscious, but is looking for his wife and thrashing about.

The nurse pulls up his chart, and orders a dose of dopamine for the anaphylactic shock. The medication has just been delivered and she is about to put it into his IV, when Jenny arrives and rushes into the room. She calls out, "Stop!" The nurse looks at her in shock. Jenny runs over and demands to know what medication she is administering. The now angry and defensive nurse replies hotly that she is giving dopamine to counter the anaphylaxis. Jenny comes unglued. "Are you trying to kill him?!" she demands. "You put that medication in his IV and he'll be dead in five minutes!" This shakes the nurse for a moment. Jenny demands that the nurse go and look at Mark's chart again. "What does it say, right there in red letters?" she shouts. 'Allergies: Dopamine,' right there in front of you."

Luckily, this story has a happy ending. Mark recovers and leaves the hospital after a couple of hours with Jenny at his side.

You may be wondering why I told I told this story. This is a story about Data Governance. Data Governance is the science and activity of ensuring that the right information is available in the right place, in the right way, at the right time, for the right reason.

In the above example, the necessary data was clearly available. But it was not governed. If it had been governed, the system would have included enforced data rules and the nurse would never have been able to order a medication that the patient was allergic to, which was clearly visible and available in the system that she was using to manage his care.

Enforced data rules are built into systems as fail-safes to avoid accidents for critical data elements or data management. They can be as dramatic as preventing administration of a drug that will cause allergic reactions or as common sense as restricting creation of duplicate records by checking against common identifiers, such as Social Security Numbers.

Failed governance, in the form of the lack of system enforced data rules that would prevent a medication from being ordered for the patient when an allergy alert is present, could have killed this patient. If Mark's wife had not been in the room when it occurred, she would have met her husband in the morgue that day.

This type of situation occurs every day all around us. Most failed governance doesn't have life or death consequences. In fact, we encounter both failed and successful governance every day. An example of successful governance happens every morning when you order your coffee and they write your name on your cup. This simple kind of governance activity ensures that you will get what you ordered and eliminates the possible mistake of the person behind the counter guessing which cup goes with which numbered order on a screen. Not life or death for most people. But important to you, the customer. And equally as important, it saves money for the coffee company by minimizing incorrect order fulfillment causing waste of products, employee time, and cups.

Data governance is an integral part of our lives. We may not realize it because we don't really know what it means to govern data. Very few organizations have robust data governance structures. Large corporations usually have many of the components, even if they are not formalized into a governance program. Small companies may have fewer components and may believe that the rigor of governance is not needed. But if the small company hopes to grow into a large organization, they would be wise to put these principles into practice from the early days of their company rather than forcing a significant change as they grow. At end of each chapter, I have created a "Small Business Corner" that helps relate the chapter to the company that is just starting out or for one that is planning to grow into a larger enterprise.

Before we go much deeper into the topic of how to set up a governance organization, we should understand why it is so necessary, and we need to have a common language and framework. Let's start with the common language and then cover why governance is so important. (Note: you will find a comprehensive Glossary indexed to page numbers in the Appendix section.)

What do you think of when you hear the terms Data Governance Committees, Rules, Policies, or Code Map? Well, governance covers all those terms and more. Here is some basic vocabulary:

- Data Governance: The activity of defining and organizing structure around information.
- Data: Information in electronic or paper form.
- Structured Data: Usually referring to data in a relational database.

- Unstructured Data: Usually referring to data in business applications such as Word, Excel, or Access, picture libraries, etc.
- Information Waste: Duplicative or proprietary data that adds confusion or does not add value to a process. Information Waste adds cost without adding value.
- Policy: A rule or set of rules that define what is acceptable or expected.
- Domain: A set of data that is related by topic. For example, a Financial Domain would be the data and information that is related to money, income, and/or accounting. A Customer Domain would be the data and information that relates to the customer including demographic data, purchasing habits, etc.
- Data Owner: Usually the individual in an organization that has the accountability for a domain of data.
- Data Steward: An individual that has been designated to care for a set of data or data processes who is accountable to the Data Owner for the proper management of the data.

- Data Custodian: Usually an Information Technologist who is accountable for the integrity of a system that holds data or information.

- Enterprise Data Governance: The structure of organization across a company, or enterprise, intended to manage and control the company's data assets and practices.

- Data Assets: The collection of data or information that provides the company with the ability to differentiate themselves in the market by leveraging the data available within their own systems, often employing Advanced Analytics. Data Assets can be quantified and, in large corporate organizations, are often part of the financial ledger of company assets.

- Advanced Analytics: The science of mining for and extracting information from many data sources for the purpose of explaining or predicting trends and/or behaviors. Common practitioners are Data Scientists or Medical Informaticists.

- Data Quality: Concerned with the level of accuracy and correctness of the data being governed; may also include any or all of the nine Data Quality Dimensions (see Chapter 7 for more on this topic).

- Metadata: Information about data. For example, #hashtags on Twitter, which help the application sort and deliver content, or counts of the number of cups of coffee sold at a diner between eight and nine in the morning.
- Data Lineage: A systematic way to classify data making it traceable through its life-cycle. This generally includes the metadata of where the information was created, managed, transferred, transformed, merged, consumed, etc.
- Big Data: Usually referring to a large collection of information in a data lake or data warehouse.
- Cloud: Information held "off-premise" or "hosted" by a third-party service provider. When combined with discussion of Big Data, the Cloud is sometimes referred to as a "virtual data lake."
- Data Lake: A collection of structured and unstructured data.

- Data Warehouse: A structured collection of data.
- On-Prem: Referring to a system holding data that is installed/held on the premise or property of the company.
- Off-Prem or Hosted: Referring to a system holding data that is installed/held in a location of a service provider and available via an internet link.

The topics and components of a data governance program may surprise you. It is made up of topics that have been used for years. If you take an inventory of your company you will find one or more (probably many) of these principles in operation: Document Management, Data Quality, Access and Security, Interoperability and Data Standards, Transformations and Integrations, Data as an Asset, Metadata, Master Data Management, and Big Data.

The most basic components include the topics that fall under the heading "Document Management." Document management includes:

- Writing, storage and categorization of policies
- Security around storage of information
- Naming conventions
- Filing systems for paper and folder structure for electronic documents
- Document retention policies

If you have ever filed papers alphabetically, you have used this kind of data governance.

Data Quality (or Information Quality) is a crucial component of data governance. As an introduction, data quality is the science of ensuring the accuracy, completeness and timeliness of information. I dedicate an entire chapter to this topic (chapter 7). The quality of information that you have access to for running your business will ultimately decide the fate of your business. It really is that important.

In this era of hackers, WikiLeaks, and internet terrorism, the topic of Security could not be more relevant. But it must also be balanced by the need for access from everywhere. More and more often our employees are mobile. They can work from anywhere and need access to the same information they would have if they were sitting in a specific physical location. Especially as we transition to an ever-expanding global economy, our workers may be onshore or offshore. They may work from home. They may be at a client site. You may have a "Bring Your Own Device" (BYOD) policy. Access and Security are integral for proper governance.

In addition to a mobile workforce, companies need many systems to run their business. The information in one system must be able to be integrated with the information in the next system along the business process/data flow. This introduces the topic of Information Lifecycle. This is the end to end journey of information from where it is originally created or managed through various transformations for use by the consumers of the information. Sometimes these transformations are so dramatic that the consumers of the information cannot recognize data at the point of creation.

The Source To Target Map (STTM) and Code Map described next can help in tracing the information. This is important when the consumers of data have errors or defects that need to be remediated. Finding the correct team or process where a problem originates is sometimes like looking for a needle in a haystack. The governance artifacts provide the map.

To integrate data, it must be structured and defined in a way that can be mapped. A component of every integration project includes a Source To Target Map (STTM), which not only defines the table and field from where the information originates (the source), it defines the target table and field, and includes definition of data type, i.e. numeric, alpha, varchar (variable character), etc., and the rules about the transformation of the data from one system to another. These rules may be as simple as "direct move." Or they may be as complex as a SQL snippet defining what to filter on, where to pull data, and how to display it. A STTM will help the development team understand how to move the information from one system to the next. The more systems your business utilizes, the more complex the transformation mapping becomes. This makes it difficult to do Root Cause Analysis when a data error is identified.

Another artifact, called a Code Map, is commonly used to help provide instructions and clarity on information from disparate sources. Code map documents contain the Master definitions and Codes used by a company and, if developed according to industry standards, will be based on International Organization for Standardization (ISO) codes, when available. Unfortunately, most code map documents, if they exist at all, are based on the original legacy system values at the time that the code map was established. This creates a situation that hampers interoperability between organizations.

Interoperability is the ability to connect business processes from one functional group to another. This may be from one business unit to the next in a single organization, or it may be connecting a business process to a third-party vendor. Anytime information must be transferred or jointly used, interoperability is at play.

The key to interoperability is common language or sufficient code map, both of which enable information to be understood by both parties. Interoperability is one of the primary benefits of data governance. *For a brief case study on Interoperability, see the appendix. An electronic copy is also available on my website: www.getgoverned.com/interoperability.

What are the other benefits of data governance? A robust data governance structure will provide a greater understanding of the information that is captured and used to run your business. Governance will improve the experience of your customers in their interactions with your employees. Happier customers will directly lead to greater employee satisfaction. It will also help your employees feel more competent and informed about their job. Information waste and inefficiencies will be reduced. You will have the ability to make better, more informed strategic decisions. And finally, you will be able to capitalize on your information as an asset for a roadmap to growth and stability.

Whether you are part of a large company or the owner of a small company, these benefits will be realized. Let's look at each one a little deeper.

Do you know what information is needed to run your company? I don't mean "know" in a 30,000-foot level of understanding. I am talking about the fundamentals. What information do your employees collect and use? Do they collect and categorize it in a common way? Do they use the same naming conventions? Is it in a place that is accessible to everyone that needs to know?

Let's do a quick exercise together to test your knowledge of how information is used at your company. The small business may use this exercise for planning these activities. Large companies should already have much of this in place.

Let's begin. Think of five functions that occur in your company. Maybe you will choose sales, or product design, or computer system implementation, or order taking. Choose one.

Think about the team that does this work; maybe it is something that you personally do for your company. What does the person or team that does this work actually do? Can you write down a basic process flow? Is there information that they need? Make a list of the information they need to do their job. If you know, describe how the information they need is sourced and stored. How organized is it? Let's look at my example.

I'm going to use a Marketing department as an example:

To generate leads for the company, the marketing department places ads, makes phone calls, collects email addresses, and sends free articles that have been written by our executives.

Imagine how difficult it would be for the marketing team if each of them had a different way of storing contact information of customers and prospects, the status or disposition of the call, what source the lead was obtained through, and the free article that was sent to the prospect.

What if each marketing team member saved the free articles with different naming conventions in their own folder or the common folder. How dysfunctional would this team be?

Governance ensures that each person accesses a common folder of articles. Each article is named in the same way.

For this example, the articles include the following information:
- Name of the person who wrote the article
- The Main Topic of the article
- The sub-topic of the article
- When it was written.

When these principles are followed the name of the article is structured like this: *Templar_Data_Quality_9Dimensions_April 2016.docx*

The name of the document tells everyone that I wrote the article, it is about Data Quality, the subtopic is the nine data quality dimensions, it was written in April of 2017 and is stored in Microsoft Word format. It would be very confusing if the title of this article did not have the date and the sub topic of "9dimensions" listed in a way that allowed searching and quick understanding of the contents.

What was your example? Can you see how something as simple as a standard naming convention improves the timeliness and cost efficiency of every department?

Think about calling your bank. How many questions and verifications do they require before a person will answer your question or provide any assistance? It's a lot! But this series of authentication questions ensures that the bank has your most complete and correct information. When you do get to talk to a person, not only do they know who you are, but they probably know why you are calling. And in a well-governed organization, you will be talking to the correct person who can solve your problem without having to transfer you to another department. This makes for a happier and more satisfying experience.

In this chapter, I have taken you on a few information journeys to help you begin to think in an end-to-end manner about data, information, and business processes. We will use the information journey method as we dive deeper into the components of data governance and how to set them up. We will cover what you already have in your organization that can be used. I'll give you a model to structure your data governance program. I will help you understand how to set Success Criteria that will resonate with you and your boss. You will get the tools to orchestrate groups, systems and processes into a comprehensive plan. We'll have a conversation about data quality and what needs to be measured and how to measure it to be aligned with best practices. We'll develop a checklist to guide your journey and help you get out of implementation mode and into operational mode. And we'll finish strong with some resources and next steps to ensure that what you built doesn't die the moment you put it on auto-pilot.

One quick note before moving on. If you have picked up this book because you have already attempted to start a program but haven't found the success that you want, I have placed a White Paper about *Common Trouble Spots When Implementing a Data Governance Program* in the Resources section of the book. It is also available on my website: www.getgoverned.com/common_trouble_spots. You may wish to start there as a guide for where to focus your attention first.

Chapter 1 Small Business Corner

This chapter should get you thinking about places in your company where you use information. If you are reading this book, chances are good that you are hoping that your small business will grow into a large business. I have literally spent tens of millions of companies' dollars helping correct data mistakes that could have been avoided if data management process had been planned instead of thrown together and patched over time.

If you will read this book with the idea of cementing successful governance into your company culture when you are a small business, and keep it part of your culture throughout your growth, you may avoid spending the money later to clean up your processes. Your growth will be smoother and you will have more control over your information assets.

This chapter has given you an introduction to the topic of Data Governance. As we go through each chapter, there will be more specific examples that will be applicable to your small business today.

Chapter 2 – My Journey

"Nothing gives you credibility like being
from out of town."
Morgan Templar

Recognition of the field of data analytics and governance is relatively new in the business world. Prior to the 1980's, the role of manager of analytics had not been elevated to Senior Leadership. As we move deeper through the Information Age and firmly into the Digital Age, companies are finding it necessary to invest in more people to do analytic and governance work, and there is a growing trend toward one or more C-Suite roles.

The Leadership Model around Data Governance and Analytics is relatively new and still growing at a fast pace. As of 2013 there were only 200 people in the world with the title Chief Data Officer (CDO). At the end of 2016 that number had grown to 2,000 internationally*. A new C-Suite role is emerging to complement the CDO – the Chief Analytics Officer (CAO). There are many more people with titles such as Data Protection Officer (DPO), Vice President of Governance and Analytics, or Vice President of Data and Information. Considering how many companies there are in the world, it is remarkable that there are so few senior leaders in this field.

*http://cdoclub.com/chief-data-officer-jobs-update-for-november-2016/

Like the evolution of the leadership model, my expertise in the field of data governance grew organically over time. My first taste of what today is considered "data governance" was in 1982 when I first learned to prepare taxes for clients. The accounting and math disciplines were easily within my wheelhouse. But adding that element of using data from forms to analyze and calculate tax obligations that complied with the Internal Revenue Service tax code guidelines was my first commercial use of strict policies about data. At the time, I wasn't thinking about data governance, as that phrase had not really been coined. Looking back, I realize how this is similar to the level of governance utilized and needed by smaller companies.

Fast forward a few years, I worked at Merrill Lynch. I was licensed to perform all stock and option trading, buy and sell stocks, options, commodities, etc., and although I am not an attorney, my specialty was the interpretation of trusts as they related to stock trading accounts. This was another learning opportunity for me to take unstructured information in the form of a legal trust text document and convert it to the specific database codes that defined the parameters of the allowed types of transactions that could be performed in the customer's trust account. One role after another in the financial industry provided rich opportunities to experience the growth of analytics and the transformation of unstructured information into structured data.

The financial industry is absolutely leading the way in governance. They were regulated early and heavily and to manage the regulatory requirements, governing and protecting data was essential. I recall sitting in my Merrill Lynch office in Salt Lake City, Utah as the Thrifts and Savings & Loan organizations were failing. The reasons behind these failures were active debates around the water cooler, and the speculation about what it meant for banks, investment firms, and the financial future of the United States had the same feel as today's discussions around the future of health care. Witnessing the consolidation of the Federal Banking Insurance organizations of both the Federal Deposit Insurance Corporation (FDIC) for Banks and the Federal Savings and Loan Insurance Corporation (FSLIC) for Saving & Loans and Thrift organizations into a single insurance organization, the FDIC, helped me realize how the security, accuracy, and structure of information can lead to great success or great failure.

Eventually my path took me into Information Technology (IT). Although I had never been formally trained, my youth had included the advantage of a family of people on the cutting edge of computers and digital technology. I will never forget the first time I saw a laptop computer with a 9.6 baud modem (yes, I said baud, something practically unfathomable in this age of Gigabaud transmissions across wireless devices). The idea that you could plug the old telephone handset into this device and transmit information across the phone line in the form of ones and zeros made sense. Much like Morse code with the series of dots and dashes to represent letters to spell out words, the binary system of computer language was part of the language we spoke at home. My transition into IT was as natural as a duck taking to water.

One of my early jobs was on a technical support line. This was the first time professionally that I was expected to develop metadata and tag documents. Each person was expected to write up a brief about the customer problems we encountered and add them into the solutions library. For that information to be usable by other agents, each document was tagged with key words (metadata) and document control numbers that identified the category (laptop, desktop, or network), the general class of the problem (hardware, software, or third-party device compatibility) and the specific problem the brief was focused on solving. Just like the financial industry, the IT industry was beginning the framework that would become analytics and data governance. Of course, there were data scientists and

Informaticists in various industries, but the concepts were still rather obscure.

Once again, the "Dot Com Bust" of 2000 was a study in the importance of governed information and data. As the Director of Process Improvement at a start-up technology company, I was able to witness first hand as one company after another failed. It was evident that security, transparency and good documentation were the difference between a viable company that weathered the collapse and one that crumbled when the market conditions changed.

In 2001, my path took me to healthcare. This was an industry that I knew very little about other than as a customer. There were certainly people in the industry with deep understanding of analytics and data mining. With a primary focus of improving the medical care of patients, the healthcare industry led the way in case studies and research into new treatment modalities. But in my experience, outside of those few people involved with research, the healthcare industry generally functioned on unstructured, paper-based information. Policies were written up and approved, but they were then distributed and filed away. I had big binders on my desk, one for each area of the company that I was accountable to, and I would replace outdated policies with the updated one as they came out. Many people just didn't bother.

Digitization of information was simply not occurring. I would spend hours, sometimes days, reading through binders of paper-based government regulation documents to find the information we needed to stay compliant.

I was asked to run my first big project in 2002. Of course, I was familiar with the idea of project management, mostly as a practice within the construction industry. But I didn't know the first thing about how to run a project. This turned into a blessing in disguise. I not only had the opportunity to build a nursing education program for the Urban Central Region of Intermountain Health Care, I had the chance to learn about the way projects are managed.

Projects run on data. If you are not familiar with project management, here is a very brief overview. Projects are managed using one of two primary methodologies: Waterfall (sometimes called Software Development Life Cycle or SDLC) or Agile (sometimes called Scrum or Kanban).

Projects have phases or sprints. These are sections of the work that need to be completed before moving on to the next segment. Usually a Phase Gate review is performed and approved before the project can get the next batch of funding or move on to the next set of tasks. All projects must complete the same steps – Planning, Design, Development, Unit Testing, Quality Assurance (QA) testing, User Acceptance Testing (UAT), Promotion through environments to Production, and finally, post go-live warranty.

A Waterfall project completes all of the steps of each of these phases before passing the Phase Gate and moving to the next phase. The Planning phase includes the business case, requirements and project plan. These artifacts are taken to the Phase Gate review and approved before moving on to the Design phase, and so on.

An Agile project usually functions in 2-week Sprints. The full lifecycle of plan, design, develop, test occurs for each user story in the sprint and is completed within the two-week period.

In both cases, the same documents are created, but in Waterfall they are written and approved within the correct phase and approved in their entirety before passing the phase gate. In Agile, the documents grow organically as the team moves through the backlog. (This is not a book on Project Management or Agile methodology. For resources on this topic, see the References section.)

I have always favored the Agile methodology. This is due, in large part, to having the opportunity to stay abreast of the birth of Agile as a framework in American project management. In February 2001, a group of developers and visionaries in the software world met at Snowbird, a ski resort in Utah. Being a native Utahan and interested in the technology world,

I followed the outcomes closely. The ideas of project management were new to me and the ideas in the Agile Manifesto resonated with my background of using documentation as a guide to keep initiatives moving forward (see References for more information on Agile). I learned about the Project Management constraint triangle of Scope, Time, and Budget. And I learned about using two-week sprints to monitor and complete the work.

My first project was to implement an accredited Registered Nurse training program. I had about twelve weeks to negotiate a contract with an accredited school (we chose a community college), find students with all prerequisites completed and conduct interviews for participation, locate a classroom site on one of our campuses and get it configured, painted and stocked, order all textbooks, write and subsequently have each student sign an agreement that in exchange for essentially free education they would agree to work for my company for the equivalent hours of the two-year program, and finally I monitored the progress of the students and served as the problem resolution department. All of this was in addition to my "day job." I simply could not have accomplished all those tasks without significant structure and utilization of the governance components of business process management, policy management, and disciplined project management. I didn't have any fancy tools; I tracked everything on a multi-tab Excel spreadsheet. I kept it ordered and on track because each task had an ID and description that was consistently applied throughout every aspect of the program. I essentially created a data lineage document, even though I would not hear the term "data lineage" for many years.

Today's project managers have much more structure, and the expectation that they will follow set procedures is universally understood. Project management, regardless of Waterfall or Agile methodology, utilizes Business Requirement Documents (BRD) with control numbers for each requirement, traceability of requirements to development work, standard status reporting, and phase gates to ensure activities stay in alignment with delivery expectations. Each of these components is an aspect of data governance. They allow for the information about each project in a company to be measured and evaluated with common standards and expectations. Project Management and the disciplined methodology promoted by the Project Management Institute (PMI) is an ideal place to look for elements of data governance.

In 2003, Intermountain Health Care brought in a consulting group that taught us the basics of the Toyota Production System and its application to the delivery of healthcare. The Toyota Production System is a method of process improvement developed in Japan beginning in the 1950's and it eventually became what we know today as LEAN, Six Sigma, or LEAN Six Sigma.

These process improvement methodologies take a statistical approach to improvement that requires data for analysis and applies standard documents and calculations to show whether a process is in control, aligned within a quality score of 99.999997% (6α, utilizing the Greek alphabet symbol for Sigma to represent a standard of deviation no more frequent or prevalent than 3 standard deviations either above or below the measure for perfection). Looking back from a position of having trained first for certification in LEAN and then for Six Sigma Black Belt certification, I recognize that the level of training we received more than a decade ago has been a foundation for my view of quality and data ever since. This basic training led to the incorporation of continuous process improvement in everything I undertook from that time forward.

The Six Sigma principles are based on statistical modeling and activities that gather and analyze data for improvement and control of processes. The data needed to perform this analysis must be consistent, relative, and sufficient. This implies a process of capturing data in either structured or unstructured formats that can be utilized to illustrate the state of efficiency of a process. Governing data is crucial for successful improvement projects. There is simple beauty in the DMAIC (Define, Measure, Analyze, Improve, Control) lifecycle that dovetails beautifully with governance. The graphs and charts used with Six Sigma, such as the Control Chart, Ishikawa "fish bone" analysis, and even simple Pareto Charts, imply an understanding and structure of information that is only possible through applying governance techniques.

Continuous Process Improvement became my mantra. Every process I encountered had waste and every structure could be Leaned-Out. I came to embody change, which is good and bad. People know what to expect, but change is uncomfortable for most people. "Change or Die" is a common phrase out of my mouth. "Entropy is death" is another.

This desire to see things improve provided an amazing opportunity at my next healthcare adventure at Coventry Healthcare. I started out as an Operations Manager in the credentialing verification center, but it quickly became apparent that I was a much better tool at implementing change management and process improvement. A very notable example was the shortening of the Contract to Credentialing to Enrollment lifecycle. Over a period of 90 days we transitioned the entire start to finish process from a 270-day turnaround time to a 90-day turnaround time. And in doing so, we improved quality scores by 15% overall.

That improvement mindset led to another amazing opportunity. At the time, my company had twenty-one health plans with membership and providers in all 50 states. The provider network was about a million providers across all plans and products. We had already implemented a process I call the "Strictest Standard" for our policies. What this entailed was working with our team of attorneys to define the data and process standards for credentialing and enrollment in all 50 states. We also evaluated the requirements of CMS (Centers for Medicare and Medicaid Services), NCQA (National Committee for Quality Assurance), and URAC (Utilization Review Accreditation Committee) and created a Standards matrix. The goal was to identify the most stringent requirement and meet that requirement for every provider in the network. It seems like an extreme approach, but it allowed us to establish a single, unified process to credential and enroll a provider. This guaranteed that regardless of which health plan the provider was contracted with or which state she practiced in, our credentialing and enrollment was sufficient for all standards.

Shortly after implementing the "Strictest Standard" program one of my analysts identified an interesting trend. Several of our health plans literally bordered each other leading to an overlap in provider participation. This analyst and I dug deeper into the data and realized that with the new standards, we could align the credentialing and recredentialing activities to a common date for all participating plans and save the time and money necessary to recredential those overlapping providers more than once in the requisite three-year cycle. Even with our aggressively low cost of $55 per credentialing event, eliminating the dual processing would save the company $7 Million over the three-year cycle.

It was easy on paper, but to implement required the approval of either the President or Vice President of Provider Services, as appropriate, along with the Chief Medical Officer for each health plan. I founded a coalition within our plans that we called the Credentialing Caucus. We met weekly and debated the merits of the change, worked through the obstacles and within a period of ten weeks, we implemented the "Single Credentialing" initiative. With $7 Million on the line, it was a big win. None of that could have been done without first establishing the tight governance of the data that was in our system: the collection methods, the method of documentation, and the standardization of business processes. These governance activities together allowed us to spot that trend and capitalize upon it.

I would be remiss if I fail to mention that there was a cost to this implementation. The attorneys did a lot of research, my analyst and I put in many 80-hour weeks, and we had the time and attention of over a hundred people including Presidents of health plans and Chief Medical Officers. After factoring in all those costs, it left a net of more than $6.5 Million in savings. I give this example so that you can begin to see methods of calculating Return on Investment (ROI) from data governance activities.

Another amazing benefit from my "Strictest Standard" methods was in the compliance with regulations and the ease with which we sailed through our audits. Each regulatory or accreditation agency has their own set of standards. And in the health care provider data world, you expect to be audited at least annually and in some cases quarterly. Having clear documentation of how our new methods incorporated the standards of each state, each accreditation agency and even the Federal CMS standards gave us the leverage to engage in an audit from a very strong position. At that point, passing audits became routine and not the mad scramble that they usually are as you prepare files for audit. We could literally pull up the electronic files and put them into a restricted access folder for the auditor to use for their audits, provide a copy of the documented rules and standards, and sit back to answer the occasional question. Audit pass rates went up by 20% in the first year.

As part of my work at Coventry, I implemented an operational project to take our department paperless. With five offices across the country, we needed to be able to share information and flex workloads between sites. We used a commercial vendor to install high end scanners in each office and used a governed indexing system. No more shipping ten-ream boxes of paper full of Personally Identifying Health Information (PHI/PII) across the country. In one single month, prior to the implementation of our paperless processes, one of those boxes was accidently delivered to the Walmart across the street from one of our offices and another box was delivered to one of our provider's offices because when UPS opened it up, his name and address were printed on the top papers in the box. Both incidents were completely accidental, but they were a breach of Privacy regulations and quite a bit of damage control had to be done. Our Executive Vice President signed the funding request for the scanners a few weeks later. The moral of this story is to capitalize on your mistakes!

Mistakes are bound to happen. We are still a world of humans, not robots. It is important to establish a method of ensuring information and data quality. It is important to realize that without information quality, data governance simply cannot succeed. Audits are critical to ensure that business processes are followed. But equally important is the need to establish business processes, workflows, policies, and job aids that support the governance activities and standards. These things are table stakes in the Digital Age. And while we will go into more detail about them, it is important to realize that most companies already do at least some of these activities. When we talk about data quality later, we'll dive into broader views of what data quality is and how to measure it.

Before we dive deeper into data quality, let's take a step back and talk about how to implement a data governance process for your organization.

Chapter 2 Small Business Corner

Many topics were briefly introduced in this chapter. The two topics that are most applicable to the small business are LEAN and Project Management.

Every business has waste. Constant improvement of your products and processes are the way to stay competitive. LEAN provides some structure and support to make improvements in a less invasive way. There are many good books and consulting services that can help you trim any fat, something critical in a small business that may be strapped for cash.

Project Management provides structure to change. Every small business at some time will need to accomplish something that requires the coordination of many resources. Using some of the tools of Project Management in a disciplined way will make those projects easier to manage and control.

A common mistake for growing businesses is to allow change to happen without a plan. Project management will supply the structure to keep your "small project" from bankrupting your small business.

Chapter 3 – Success Criteria

"If you aren't in over your head,
how will you know how tall you are?"
T.S. Elliot

Data Governance requires that information is actively managed. This includes, at the very least, metadata management, business impact analysis, data quality, and policy compliance. Before diving into the "How" section of setting up a Data Governance program, it is critical to establish the "What" or outcomes you will use to measure your progress and ultimate success. In the vein of Stephen Covey's, "begin with the end in mind," you need to understand what your boss and your company executives will consider *success*. Your goal, of course, will be to knock the ball so far out of the park that there will be no doubt that you are the superstar!

Many governance programs have great initial progress, but in the end, are considered failures because the program put into place was not sustainable. Don't do that! The most successful governance programs are those that have a few things in common: clear outcomes, executive buy-in, cross functional participation, and a plan that includes milestones and objectives.

Your Success Plan will need to include the expected outcomes, the method to measure benefits, the breadth of the program, the funding constraints, the expected timelines for each outcome, and named accountable parties. If you are a project manager, you just heard me say, "Charter, Benefits, Scope, Budget, Timelines, Milestones, Stakeholders, Roles and Responsibilities, and Project Sponsor." It is absolutely critical that you understand, and continually remind yourself, that no success is possible without buy-in from the key people at every level and at every step. Don't get frustrated by this. It is part of the process.

Remember that everyone has other priorities and this will feel like more bureaucracy at first. Only mature programs that are well established begin to see the lessening of resistance. Some experts in the field of data governance will tell you that it is possible to establish non-invasive programs. This is only true after governance becomes part of the culture. Data governance is extremely invasive during implementation because it must be inserted into every department, process, system and corner of your business. Of course, that is only true if you want a program that will be sustainable. Starting small and limiting the exposure is only a good idea for a beta program.

Eventually, the governance program will be a normal part of your company culture and only new people will need to be initiated to understand and follow the program. At that point, governance will be "just the way we do things," which is quite non-invasive. Remember, though, that refreshing the importance for everyone on a regular basis, perhaps as part of annual training, keeps people engaged. Governance is not a once-and-done initiative; it is a change of culture. And that requires regular maintenance.

There is a reason that I included Project Management in the discussion. While you may not be formally trained as a project manager, the principles used in project management are not only applicable, but extremely useful to provide the structure and measurement of your end-state program and the set-up process. If you are not personally a project manager, I recommend engaging one to keep track of the many steps that need to occur. If your program is complex, hiring an expert in the field as a consultant or mentor will bring experience to the process that you may not have in your organization today. Having a mentor/consultant and a project manager working through the detailed milestones will give you, the driver of this awesome new program, the time to focus on strategy, communication, and being the face of success.

Using a simple mnemonic, MAP IT OUT, you can ensure that you have a good plan for each step.

Measurable: Specific Goals have data points that can be quantified and measured.

Achievable: Goals should be reasonable in terms of time, resources, technology or capability.

Planned: Determine the order, set priorities, have targets.

Impactful: A Cost, Time or Other benefit should be tied to the objectives.

Timely: Priorities should align with timetables. Do you have items that impact "open enrollment?" Complete those within a timeline to support the date. Have items that are dependencies for projects? Align priorities to be done when needed for testing.

Outcome Oriented: Know what you are hoping to achieve before making the plan. Always put value-add things ahead of nice-to-have.

Understandable: The plan and outcomes should be easy for anyone to grasp. Overly complex topics need to be broken down into smaller pieces.

Transparent: Have a method and a plan to report progress, blocking issues, and successes.

To help keep your program organized, I offer a step-by-step outline below. This is available to download in editable format on my website. www.getgoverned.com/success_checklist

This checklist will provide some structure for the planning and development of your program, but also allow you to customize the steps that are right for your organization. (These steps assume that you work for a large, complex corporation. The small business will need a pared down version of a governance program, and your checklist will reflect that.)

Program Success Checklist

Follow these 16 steps to develop a
World Class Data Governance Process!

Before you begin, read steps 11 & 15. Make sure operations is part of your plan from the beginning.

- ☐ Step 1: Create Draft Charter Document – include all your assumptions and expectations as a place to start getting input from stakeholders
- ☐ Step 2: Meet with each sponsor or executive leader and get their input to the Charter
- ☐ Step 3: Use feedback from sponsors to get to a Working Charter
- ☐ Step 4: Identify the broader group of stakeholders

☐ Step 5: Review the Working Charter document with Stakeholders and include their feedback

☐ Step 6: Identify any competing or conflicting interests and resolve

Steps 7 – 11 are planning the implementation items

☐ Step 7: Sketch out the organization structure

☐ Step 8: Define milestones

☐ Step 9: Break milestones into specific deliverables

☐ Step 10: Begin a document to capture and "parking lot" and long-term Roadmap items.

☐ Step 11: Begin the Turn-over-to-operations plan

Step 12 is a Pre-Implementation step

☐ Step 12: Hold a joint review session with sponsors and stakeholders of the Working Charter for Approval by Sponsors and Informing Stakeholders.

Implementation Steps

☐ Step 13: Complete the activities to accomplish what was planned in steps 7 – 11

☐ Step 13A: Implement the Governance Organizational Structure

☐ Step 13B: Achieve each deliverable according to schedule

☐ Step 13C: Mark off each milestone through a Phase Gate review

☐ Step 13D: Keep the Parking Lot current and begin to put in future dates for planning

☐ Step 13E: Develop the long-term Roadmap to implement items outside of the initial scope
☐ Step 13F: Develop the artifacts and staffing model needed for the Operational Model

Wrap-up and Continuity
☐ Step 14: Communicate successes, risks, issues, and status along the way
☐ Step 15: Turn over to Operations (This process varies at every organization. Make sure you know what it means for you before you even begin.)
☐ Step 16: Document your success and get your sponsor to "approve" demonstrating that you met expectations.

Now Celebrate!

We will cover each of these steps in greater detail later. For now, keep them in mind as you read through the topics in this chapter. You may wish to jot down your first impressions of what each step means to you now as a basic plan. But before you can finalize the plan, you need some additional information.

Once you have the basics of the program planned, you will need the awareness of how change affects your organization. Change management is a crucial step, and the one we will cover next.

Change Management

Companies, in fact industries, have different tolerance levels for change. Finance, at least today, tends to embrace competitive improvement in the race to make more money and beat the competition. Health care, on the other hand, tends to be much more conservative, slow to adopt change and very risk averse. It is important to understand the level of change management that will need to be undertaken. The same steps will be followed, but in a risk tolerant organization, you will likely fly through them much quicker to affect the change but the processes established may not "stick." In a risk averse organization, getting the wheel rolling may take Herculean effort. But once you crest the top of the mountain, the operational processes will roll along smoothly.

Understanding your corporate culture and the pressures of your industry will guide you in structuring your program for maximum benefit and satisfaction. See *Figure 1* for an exercise to identify your Company Risk Tolerance. For additional insight, visit www.getgoverned.com/risk_assessment to access a tool to aid you in placing your key stakeholders in the right risk category.

Figure 1 – Risk Assessment

You will need to identify the stakeholders in your organization. Make your stakeholder list and assign each one a relative risk category score. You do this by deciding how influential each stakeholder will be on implementation and for long-term culture shift. Assign a score to each stakeholder using a scale of -5 to 5 with zero being neutral and +/- 5 being very impactful. Then plot them into the correct quadrant. The interactive "personality test" on my website will help you with this assessment by asking you to choose between words when thinking about how each stakeholder acts. It will give an "X" and "Y" axis score for each person.

If you are doing the assessment manually, use the following phrase to help you score each stakeholder. Plot the score as an (X,Y) coordinate on a graph.

"(Stakeholder name)___ ranks a score of __(#)__ for implementation and a score of __(#)__ for culture shift. they fall in _(Quadrant)_."

Following the example for this exercise, you will assign a value to each group of stakeholders that places them into a quadrant using the following scale:

1. This group is Agile (easy to motivate) but Risk Averse (careful about change).
2. This group is Agile (easy to motivate) and Risk Tolerant (open to change).
3. This group is Steady (hard to motivate) but Risk Tolerant (open to change).
4. This group is Steady (hard to motivate) and Risk Averse (careful about change).

Think about each stakeholder. Their Agility score will influence how supportive of change they are and how easy they will be to motivate to support the change. The Risk score is an indicator of how liberal or conservative they are culturally (and I don't mean politics). Are they going to support and model the changes after implementation to help the change become part of the culture? Risk Tolerant people see change as an opportunity, and Risk Averse people see change as a gamble.

Culture of Change Matrix (example)

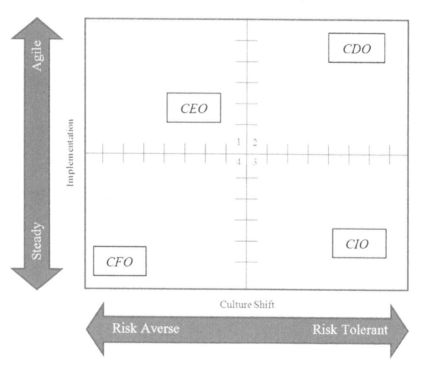

Example: The CEO is -3 for culture shift and 2 for implementation = (-3, 2) plotted in

Quadrant 1. She is moderately willing to change but conservative in Risk. The CFO is a -5 for culture shift, a -5 for implementation. He is resistant to change and conservative for Risk (-5, -5) plotted in Quadrant 4. The Chief Data Officer (CDO) is a 5 for culture shift and 5 for implementation. She is very willing to change and very Risk Tolerant (5,5) plotted in Quadrant 2. The CIO is a 5 for culture shift, a -4 for implementation (5,-4) and plotted in Quadrant 3.

End Figure 1

Having completed your key stakeholder risk analysis, you now have a picture of your culture of change. You should also have an idea of which stakeholders are critical to success. I am assuming that you understand change management to a degree. But if you would like a refresher, you will find a guide to Change Management on my website at www.getgoverned.com/change_management and in the References section of the book.   With this understanding of your key stakeholders, you can now begin to plan your success strategy.

Define the Outcomes

What is it that your company hopes to achieve through the implementation of Data Governance? It may be that the Chief Data Officer has an understanding that control of information and data, achieved through governance, is an enabling component of efficient data operations. Perhaps there is a belief that the quality or accuracy of data is poor and that the best path to improving it is to establish governance. Maybe your CEO just returned from a large national conference and heard the latest buzz word and wants to be on the cutting edge.

Whatever the reason you have been asked to put together a governance program, it is important to meet with the leader who is sponsoring the idea and really understand what it is they hope for as an outcome. If you are driving data governance from a "bottom-up" perspective, you will need to understand what will motivate one or more of your executives to sponsor the program. You should be hearing a common theme – you need an executive sponsor if you are going to be successful in a wide-spread or enterprise initiative. Ideally you will have the backing of the entire cross-functional leadership team. If you are only implementing governance for a single business unit, you will, at the very least, need the support of your immediate leaders.

Establish the Charter

The Charter document will provide the structure to ensure understanding of the initiative and frame the conversations with your leadership and stakeholders. It is the beginning of your success plan and forms the common understanding of the expected outcomes for all parties. The formal approval of a charter is an agreement of sorts – it documents the name and date of the approver, shows understanding of the scope, and gives you the authority to undertake the effort on behalf of the company. Depending on your company standards, the Charter may be all that is needed or you may expand the Charter to a full Business Case. I won't cover business cases here because if one is necessary, you will need to comply with your company standards. See Figure 2 for a Charter template.

Figure 2 – Charter Template

<u>Name of Initiative:</u> For example, Data Governance at XYZ Corporation.

<u>Objective or Goal:</u> *Describes the expected outcomes or scope in clear, concise language.*

<u>Participants:</u> *Names the primary parties involved. May be in a table format. Should include at least: Executive Sponsor/Program Owner; Program Driver; Project Manager, if applicable. Some organizations require both a business and IT representative in each of these roles. If governed under a specific internal organization, that would be listed here. i.e. Quality Improvement, Build the Foundation, End-to-End Flow, etc.*

<u>Stakeholders:</u> *These are the people who will be impacted, involved, or need to know about the progress of the initiative.*

<u>Requirements:</u> *These may be specific or general. For a Charter, I recommend that they are fairly broad in nature. For a Data Governance program, you may include things such as:*

- *The program must include representation from all departments (or data domains or business units, as applicable).*
- *Policies will be established that cover topics such as data usage, common definitions, data standards, data asset management, data quality expectations, etc.*
- *A governing body will be established with clearly defined roles and responsibilities, structure of committees, frequency of meetings, rules, etc.*
- *Resources needed for implementation will be defined.*
- *Resources for ongoing operations will be established.*

<u>Constraints or Risks:</u> *Defines any perceived roadblocks, challenges, boundaries or items to overcome. For example, "Risk: Resources will*

not be available." "Constraint: The Governance Body will not make decisions about systems; these decisions belong to Enterprise Architecture."

Assumptions: *Describes the expectations that are generally understood to be true. Essentially, this section helps define operating norms. Such as, "It is assumed that identified data steward resources will be allocated sufficient time to engage in the expected governance activities." Or, "It is assumed that the Steering Committee will set the direction and the Stewards Council will implement."*

Milestones: *Assumes you know the expected end state and specific things that must be done to achieve it. Documents the expected timelines to complete major deliverables or outcomes. Helps define checkpoints for ongoing activities.*

Communication: *Describes the method and frequency that updates will be provided to leadership and stakeholders. Describes the method of interaction between groups, for example if you have a Steering Committee and a Stewards Council, how they will engage in two-way communication. May also define how general communications occur to the broader company audience and/or specific groups, such as analytic teams when policies or decisions will affect them.*

Deliverables: The specific artifacts that are expected to be generated by the program. Examples include an organization chart, communication plan, policies for X, Y, or Z, etc. Usually these specific deliverables will have Milestone dates.

Approvals: Lists the specific approvers of the Charter by name and includes the date of approval. Implies that they have reviewed and provided feedback. This is the "contractual" element of the Charter.

End Figure 2

Make a Plan

Now that you know what should be included in a Charter document, you are ready to begin formulating the plan for execution (remember that the checklist that was given on page 50 is also available as an editable document on my website at www.getgoverned.com/success_checklist). Let's go into more detail on each of the steps:

Step 1: Fill out your Draft Charter document. You will need to start with documenting your personal vision and ideas. This is just a place to start. People are always better at editing than they are at coming up with original ideas.

Step 2: Meet with each of the Sponsors and key participants. This isn't everyone who will be part of the program, these are the leaders and drivers. Ask them for their perspective on each of the Charter components. Find out why they are interested in establishing Data Governance. What are their key motivators? What does success mean to them; what is their vision? Who do they see as key contributors? Is there anyone that they could imagine might be a blocker? How would they approach a conversation with that person to help them see the vision? Is there any funding available for the program? Do they have a perspective or a resource in mind to help frame the structure? i.e. Are they following an industry model? Or have they spoken with a vendor?

Step 3: Take all the interview feedback and compile it into a single Working Charter draft document. It is helpful to have structured your interviews around the charter and to fill in the information in each section for each stakeholder. When you combine the feedback into each section to develop clear and concise statements of scope, you will inevitably identify statements that don't align. Those might be the gems that make your program special or they may be noise that needs to be quieted to be successful.

Step 4: Identify the group of Stakeholders. This is a much broader group of people than your sponsors or drivers. This includes every leader, or their representative, who will be impacted by the scope of the program. This group of people will have the details of how the program will impact them.

Step 5: Inform the stakeholders that they have been identified to participate and provide them with an overview of the program. Don't expect them to get it at first, but be prepared to provide both the intent and scope of the program. Try to personize it for each of them and give them the perspective of your sponsors about the stakeholder's role. Depending on your corporate culture, it may be important for you to meet with each stakeholder individually first or you might start with a big stakeholder kickoff and meet with them individually afterward. Either method will work, but you should plan both individual sessions and a group session to ensure that everyone hears the same information. Get their feedback of the Working Charter and incorporate it into the document. It may be helpful to keep some notation that separates Sponsor feedback from Stakeholder feedback. Ultimately, the program must meet the Sponsor's expectations, but will only be successful if the Stakeholders buy into it.

Step 6: Identify if you have competing or conflicting interests from your interviews. If you find that you do, the recommended approach is to meet with the parties that disagree and facilitate a conversation to get aligned in purpose. Use your best judgement about whether this is a conversation with just the two that conflict or if you think that this is a more significant issue that warrants a conversation with the leadership team first. It is very important that you get full alignment and a consistent message from your leadership team at this step for a couple of reasons. First, your milestones and deliverables will be based on the expectations of your leadership team, so you will need to be consistent. Second, once you expand the conversation to your broader Stakeholder audience, you will most certainly have some competing interests. Having alignment and backing from your leadership will help you navigate those conflicts.

Step 7: Plan your program organization structure. Chapter five provides detailed information about the potential Roles and Responsibilities for a governance program. Read through those definitions, decide what makes the most sense for your organization and put together a draft organization chart.

Step 8: Define milestones. The milestones are the big picture headings, or the "What," and deliverables are the sub-headings, or the "How," of what you want to accomplish. These can be broken down into Topics, Phases, Data Domains, or other division depending on the structure of your program. Think of Milestones as Chapter Headings in a book.

Step 9: Break milestones into specific deliverables. The deliverables may be as granular as a step-by-step guide or they may be defined as specific artifacts that will be created, reviewed, or delivered. The deliverables, more than any other step, will help set the Timelines. Remember the project management triangle here – scope, time, and money. Less time will mean either less scope or more money. At this stage, you don't need to completely plan those artifacts. Just understand what they are, how you plan to approach them, and about how long they will take. (We'll cover each of them in detail, later.)

Step 10: Begin a document to hold ideas for a long-term roadmap. This is a parking lot item at this stage. Things will come up that are not in your specific plan or scope for the initial implementation. Or they may take longer than you are given for Phase One. These get placed on a Roadmap. Once you have a list of things for future inclusion, you will begin to see or create a logical sequence. Put those on a Roadmap document. By the end of your initial implementation, you should have at least at two-year, and preferably a three-year, Roadmap that will be developed in conjunction with the Executive Steering Committee and Enterprise Architecture/IT long-term business and technical roadmaps.

Step 11: Sketch out the Operational Model. Will the data governance organization need fully dedicated people? Will it be an assignment for each data domain to send representation? Who will lead it? How do you keep the things you have implemented from fading away after you personally stop driving them? We'll go into detail on the Operating Model in Chapter 8.

Step 12: Review the Charter document with your Sponsoring Leadership team and Stakeholders. For best results, make this a joint review for a couple of reasons; first, you only need to answer questions once, and second, questions or comments from one person may spark another person with a golden idea – don't miss the opportunities. Document any questions and suggested changes. Ensure they are covered in your Charter. Some organizations will ask you to meet with the Stakeholders again before finalizing the Charter. Some may recommend collaborating with the Data Stewards before finalizing the Milestones and /or Deliverables. The important thing is that you know the path to take before getting final approvals. Send the Charter to the leadership team for approval. Once you have that approval, you are ready for implementation. That is covered in Step thirteen.

Step 13: Complete the activities to accomplish what was planned in steps 7 – 11:

Step 13A: Implement the Governance Organizational Structure

Step 13B: Achieve each deliverable according to schedule

Step 13C: Mark off each milestone through a Phase Gate review

Step 13D: Keep the Parking Lot current and begin to put in future dates for planning

Step 13E: Develop the long-term Roadmap to implement items outside of the initial scope

Step 13F: Develop the artifacts and staffing model needed for the Operational Model

Step 14: Communicate successes, issues, risks, decisions, and status regularly. This takes us back to those project management best practices. Regular status reports should be prepared and submitted to the steering committee.

As you work through these steps, a RAID document should be created and maintained. RAID stands for Risks, Action Items, Issues, and Decisions. Keeping track of each of those items along with date opened, by whom, who is responsible to resolve, and disposition of each item will give you a helpful tool to have traceability of the decisions made, the level of participation based on assigned and completed action items, and the risks and issues that may need a sponsor or stakeholder to help mitigate or remove.

Step 15: Complete documentation and plan the turn-over to Operations. This sounds like the final step, but there are a few additional components. First is to define the model for operations. Second is to ensure that appropriate funding and/or staff are allocated for success. Third is to define what ongoing success looks like. Fourth, the governing structure of committees and approvals must be documented and understood. Finally, the Roadmap should be completed and ready to be transitioned to the leader of the operational process to implement and be accountable to drive. These steps sound a lot like the initial implementation steps for a reason. You are setting up processes that will be a circle of continual monitoring and improvement.

Step 16: Conduct the turn-over to operations. This will likely include both delivery of documentation and the appropriate training to ensure continuity.

Step 17: Document your success! Get approval and sign-off from Sponsor that you achieved your outcomes and have successfully met the objectives. Make sure your boss is fully aware and that feedback is communicated through her. You deserve the credit for setting up an amazing program. Don't miss this opportunity!

Step 18: Celebrate! I don't mean that figuratively. Literally collect the key individuals and plan a celebration. This is a crucial step in leading any change. The more celebrations are built around milestones, the more excited the team will be to achieve them. It is absolutely a motivational tool. But don't be the unsung hero. Be willing to take the credit for leading this effort. You will do more things in the background than anyone will know. Humbly take credit and thank those who made it possible.

Next, we will go a little deeper into some of the above steps in this chapter. Some of the steps warrant their own chapter and will be covered later.

Meet with Stakeholders

With your Charter written and at least conditionally approved, it is time to meet with the Stakeholders. Corporate culture will play an important part in this process. There are two basic models, and it is important for you to be aware of this for maximum success.

Some organizations like a more organic approach. In this model, you would meet with each stakeholder group individually, or perhaps even the specific key individual. Socialize the ideas. Feel them out. Help them get past any resistance before they must represent their group in a large meeting. This may be a company-wide approach, or it may be necessary only with a few individuals, especially those in the Steady/Risk Averse quadrant 4.

The other approach is to call all the stakeholders together for a Kick-off meeting where the participants may be hearing about this initiative for the first time.

Kick-off Meetings

Kick-off meetings are important every time you expand the conversation. It is very important that your kick-offs with each group include a few key components. If you have meetings that follow a cascading model of more and more focused discussion from leadership down to implementation resources, only the immediate leader of the audience needs to participate.

For example, the first kick-off should be with the Sponsoring Executive and the Driver and should include the heads of the business units or functional areas/Domains – discussion will be broad and strategic. The next meeting may be with the designated Data Stewards who will be assigned by the heads of each business unit or Domain. In that meeting, their leaders should be present. Logistically, these might be done one Domain at a time. Discussion will get more tactical with each level step-down.

The next kick-off may be a combined meeting of the Data Stewards from all Domains. I would recommend that you bring the Sponsoring Executive in for this meeting and invite the Domain leaders as optional participants.

- The sponsoring leader should attend.
- You, as the Driver, should provide an overview of the program.
- The Sponsoring Executive or Domain leader should express their expectation of support and cooperation.
- You provide an explanation of why their support is needed.
- Provide a description of the specific resource asks.
- Offer a commitment to a communication plan, including method and schedule – in person, by email, on company intranet, blog, etc.
- A Buy-In moment, when you ask for their support and get their affirmative answer.

Each of the meetings you have should be documented in notes or formal minutes, depending on company norms, and include taking of attendance and any Decisions or Commitments made during the meeting.

Pro Tip: Engage a scribe responsible to take notes and/or record the sessions. It is important for you to be able to focus on the conversation and be present in the moment, not struggling to keep up with typing. There may also be people who missed the meeting who would benefit from listening to the recording. But know your company policy and/or state guidelines about recording beforehand.

Milestones

This is where the rubber meets the road and is arguably the most difficult part of setting up a Governance program. Milestones mark incremental improvement. The reason it is so challenging is because each organization has different reasons for initiating a governance program and different expected outcomes. If you are a very experienced program manager, this section may be a little redundant. But for most of us, this isn't a skill we practice often.

The best place to start is to give you a framework for how to breakdown an expected outcome into parts and then estimate the amount of time you guess it will take to accomplish.

Figure 3 – Outcomes

If you have ever written a User Story for an Agile project, you have done this. It looks like:

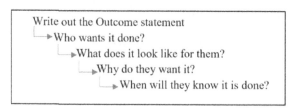

If there is more than one "Who, What, Why or When" repeat the steps for each of them. Use the structure of this example:

Outcome: *Establish a standard method of policy writing and documentation.*

Who: *As manager for the consulting team*

What: *I need my team to follow standard policy construction and numbering systems that* *includes topic, date, numbering system, and approving parties*

Why 1: *So that my policies can be stored in the central repository, and*

Why 2: *I will not have policies that differ from other teams for the same topic*

When: *I will know I am done when my team has fully adopted the new system.*

Stated as a sentence: *"As a manager of the consulting team, I need to ensure that all policies written for and by my department/team adhere to the company Policy Writing Standards so that my policies can be stored in the central storage repository AND so that they may be searchable to eliminate redundant or conflicting policies. I will know I am done when my team has fully adopted the new system."*

End Figure 3

As demonstrated in *Figure 3*, for every outcome in your Charter, you should be able to identify the

Who, What, Why, and When. In the example, the Who doesn't matter, it could be one or many groups. But the What and Whys do matter. And you may need different milestones for each one.

Remember that you don't need every step documented for your plan. You may give a business analyst a checklist with every question to ask and every step to take to get the user story documented, but you may not need to go that extreme if you or your analyst is a skilled at eliciting requirements.

In order to put your plan together and establish a timeline, you need to know how many What's you have for each outcome. And if you have many Who's, you may want to build in extra time for implementation.

These are the basic structures of a milestone:
- State the expected outcome.
- Count how many What's are needed to accomplish the outcome.
- Factor in how many Who's will need to be engaged.

- Assign a period of time for developing and implementing each What with all Who's.
- Decide what can be done concurrently and what must be done in linear fashion.

Then ask a couple of dependency questions:
1. Do we need any infrastructure (people, process, or technology) to implement this outcome?
2. If so, is it in place?
3. If not, how long will it take to implement? And, Is this a dependency for the entire set of works to begin or is it only a dependency to finish the work?

Once you have done this exercise for every expected Outcome, you will have a pretty good idea of what needs to be done and how long it will take. Plot it out in Microsoft Project or use Excel or Visio to create a Gantt chart. If you know MS Project, you can assign dependencies and get a really accurate view of Timeline and Milestones. But if you don't know MS Project, don't panic and don't think you must learn it.

Either find someone in your organization who can help you set it up or just manually do it in Excel or Visio. When using Excel or Visio, make sure you call out dependencies and align your start and end dates. It is not difficult, it just takes an eye for detail. If that isn't you, find somebody to help you.

Another important reminder is that some of the What's needed to achieve your outcomes already exist in your organization. Not everything will need to be built from scratch. Take an inventory of what you know and what assets the company has. Ask each stakeholder or Steward if they have or use something that supports the outcome. You may be surprised at the pockets of governance you will encounter. Just a word of caution here, though. The existence of a similar process or policy does not mean it fully meets the outcome. Approaching those areas with an attitude of "you are almost there" may insult them, or they may be resistant to an incremental change. Understand your audience and craft your messages accordingly.

Status Reports and Dashboards

The main purpose of status reports and dashboards is to hold people accountable to action. There is an old saying, "What gets measured improves, and what gets measured and reported publicly improves faster." Nobody likes to get exposed as a weak link, nor do they want to have their team called out as difficult or slow to adopt. Reporting progress, risks and issues makes it impossible for the "blocker" to go unnoticed. It is, unfortunately, sometimes the only way to move a "mossy stone."

Several years ago, I worked on an initiative to improve the cycle time to onboard a provider into a health plan. This entails the contracting, credentialing, enrollment and pricing configuration to make the provider "claim ready." As part of that initiative the workflows of those teams were mapped out in a Rapid Process Improvement (RPI) methodology. It was identified that certain data elements were being redundantly verified by more than one team. The cost and time implications were documented and it was determined that the credentialing team was the area that needed to modify their process. Unfortunately, their manager was extremely change averse. I jokingly called him our "mossiest stone" referencing "a rolling stone grows no moss." We began reporting our progress on a status report. It became very apparent who was blocking progress. It was not very long before the Vice President of that area made staffing changes. This is an unfortunate event, but it is a direct result of transparency. And in the end, it was better for the company that this change was made.

During the Implementation phase of establishing governance, it is relatively easy to report the status of the initiative. Dashboards are generally intended to show long-term metrics and the "health" of the program.

Status report formats are often dictated by the company. In general, they will follow this model:

Executive summary: *High level overview of the activities noting only the most significant accomplishments, risks or issues.*

Status: *Provides a visual Health Indicator: Green = On Track, Yellow = At least one deliverable is at Risk to meet the deadline, Red = One or more major deliverables is expected to miss the deadline.*

Milestones: *Often a table that lists upcoming major milestones and due dates. Sometimes includes a Status indicator for each one. Sometimes a percent complete is entered, as well. This is my preferred method because you get a view of progress that is concurrent, not just linear. If not using MS Project to track milestones and dependencies, a percent complete could be a subjective number provided by those working on that milestone.*

Commentary: *Summarized statement explaining any status other than Green. Often referred to as "Path back to Green."*

Recent Accomplishments: *Bulleted, single-line mention of important activities accomplished in* *the last reporting period (month, two-weeks, or whatever schedule you are reporting on)*

Planned Activities: *Preview of the next few items to be undertaken in the upcoming reporting period.*

Action Request, Risks/Issues, or Blockers: *Some organizations use this section to request intervention or support for a specific Risk or Issue that is blocking the team from completing deliverables.*

Once established, status reports provide a rolling picture of the overall progress toward achieving the outcomes specified in the charter. They are an important part of the communication plan. They can usually be distributed widely, although some organizations prefer to keep them within a central organization. If this is the case at your company, you may need to also create a Communication Status for distribution to a broad Stakeholder group.

Dashboards, on the other hand, are intended to provide a picture of progress toward goals and outcomes, rather than the more tactical Milestones. A Dashboard may cover a broad range of topics and may require some statistical capabilities to show the important metrics and progress toward a goal. Dashboards generally are developed after the initial implementation of a program when reports have been developed, metrics established, and targets set.

Dashboards can follow a couple of different models. One model is a Visualization model. Using some kind of data visualization software, data is converted to bubble charts showing how big and how frequent an Issue is compared to other Issues, bar charts and pie graphs are used to show the percentage of reasons why data may be in or out of alignment or the progress toward a specific goal, such as data quality scores.

The other common type of Dashboard is more statistical in nature. These may include control charts to show how in or out of control a process is and whether or not the process in on track. They may also use other tools, very common in the Six Sigma framework, that demonstrate how close to "on target" each component may be. Pareto charts may be included to highlight the primary areas of opportunity. Scatter plots may show the incidents that are logged against a system or process. The kind of dashboard developed depends on how technical the audience is that will be reading the Dashboard.

When I teach courses in setting up Data Governance Programs we spend some time working through the various components of dashboards, and I can provide some basic tools and templates for generating some of the charts that were mentioned above. Alternatively, you may wish to engage a consulting company including mentors, project managers and a Six Sigma Master Black Belt, to assist your company in the development of a Data Governance program.

The Success Plan that you have now created will guide you through the immediate and longer-term steps to take. Ultimately, you want to prove to your boss and everyone else that YOU ROCKED THIS!!

Chapter 3 Small business corner

This chapter covered a lot of ground and may have seemed overwhelming to you. If you are feeling overwhelmed, it is very important that you slow down and digest each of the concepts covered in this chapter.

The main reason that Data Governance programs are not started when businesses are small is because they are, by their very nature, a method to put controls around complex ideas and structures. Managing the complex steps before your business becomes large will set you up for smoother growth of your business. Let's recap the most important points and some strategies to slim them down to the size of your business.

You only need to remember one thing, make governance a required part of your culture when your company is small and it will grow along with your company.

Project Management: When you run a small business, you usually won't use a formal project management methodology. As I like to say, at this point it is just called "work." Setting up the structure of how work gets done to always consider the project management triangle of Scope, Time, and Budget will ensure that deadlines are hit, finances are managed, and the objectives are achieved.

Success Criteria: The steps on the checklist were covered in greater detail under the "Make a Plan" section of Chapter 3. They will be the same for the small or complex business, but remember that checking the box should be simple for a small business. Reuse this checklist as you do your annual evaluation of the governance program and expand as needed.

Change Management: There are many books written on change management. It is a critical topic, and one that I encourage you to explore further. In this area, the small business is at a distinct advantage. Managing change is easier to do when you have fewer players.

Putting good change management practices into

place early in your business is another tool that will smooth the rough spots as your company grows.

Defining the outcomes: This should be very simple. You are looking for good practices that will help your business avoid some of the many pitfalls that occur during growth. Think about that as a starting point, and then define some specific things you would like to accomplish at this point.

Charter: You will need a Governance Charter. This can be a single paragraph, if you wish. Just cover each of the points in one or more sentences. The governance organization is going to be very small, maybe just you or one of your partners, at first. But write it with the idea that as your company grows, governance will be revisited at least annually and expanded to cover the new areas of your business.

Make the plan: This is the point to pull up that checklist and go through each step as described. When you are done, you will have a blueprint for governance at your company that will grow along with the size and complexity of the business.

Chapter 4 – Quick Wins

"You grab the low-hanging fruit first, such that you make a big improvement and still have funds to fix other things, if we can simply point out the small targets and show the most value for money, it's more likely they'll get funded."
Bjørn Lomborg

Now that you have identified Success, it is time to get some quick wins. Nothing supports success like success. I have briefly touched on the fact that every organization has some of the components of success already implemented. Take advantage of that. Make sure that you look in every nook and cranny to find them. And give people credit for their good practices. This will strengthen people's commitment to the overall program if they feel acknowledged and appreciated for leading the way in an area. Following are some areas where quick wins are often found. You will have others in your company.

Policies

The very first place to look for quick wins is policies. Most companies have many policies that cover a lot of topics. We must differentiate here between a Policy and a Desk Level Procedure (DLP).

A Policy tells you what the requirement is and why it is a requirement. A Desk Level Procedure (DLP) tells you how to do a task, often in minute detail. The policy may be implied by the action, but it is rarely fully spelled out.

In a recent experience, a team being audited was asked to produce a policy document for the State that would be used as part of the response to adverse findings in an audit. The operations manager that was affected handed over a stack of several hundred DLP's. They did not have a single document that spelled out their rules, policies nor how any of their procedures supported the rather significant regulatory and accreditation requirements with which they were expected to comply. Getting that document generated for their audit required two of their top analysts to essentially sequester themselves for about 40 hours. This was just for a single department, not the entire company's policies.

Hopefully this story is not resonating with you and your company already has a good foundation of written policies. The quick win here is to identify them and establish a written governance framework for current and future policies.

A well governed catalog of policies ensures that policies are written in such a way that if the only contact someone had with your company was your polices, they could read them and understand the general functions of each department. If they are well written policies, the end-to-end flow of information would be governed by policies.

A policy should include at least the following components:

Header section contains items 1 – 7, below:
   1. Name of the policy – this should be descriptive enough to stand alone.

2. A Category, Class or Business Unit description. Examples of a Category might be "data management" or "facility security." Examples of Classes include "Data," "Process," "Regulatory Compliance." The least sophisticated of the three is to designate policies by business unit such as "human resources," "internal communications," or "application development." I recommend that your end state Policy Library utilizes either Categories or Classes, preferably both.

3. Policy identification number or Document Control number – you may assign these randomly or they may be "smart coded" to indicate the class, topic, version, and/or date of the policy, as applicable.

4. Topic – Brief description or categorization of the policy, such as "Credentialing Primary Source Verification Policy."

5. What Regulations or Accreditation Standards are covered by this Policy.

6. Approval Date, Approver's Name, Owner's Name (person accountable for maintaining or updating the policy) and Version of the Policy.

7. Optionally, the header may contain a reference to the DLP's that describe how to do the work covered by the policy.

Body of the Policy:

- Begin by referencing the Regulation, Standard, or business problem that this policy addresses.

- Describe who is expected to adhere to this policy. Is it company-wide or specific to a team?

- Detail of the policy with enough reference to how it meets the standard as possible.

<u>Impacted business units:</u>

- o If more than one business unit is expected to comply with the policy, list the business unit name(s) and the numbers/names of specific DLP's governed by this policy. This section would hold descriptions of how each part of the policy is met by which team.

<u>Footer</u>

- o A footer that appears on every page that includes the policy name, version/date, and control number.

After reading the policy it should be apparent why the policy was written, who is responsible to adhere to the policy, how the policy helps meet standards or regulations, and when the policy was written and approved. It should also be easy to search on the header information of the document to find just the right policy when it is needed.

If you already have mature policies and document control, this is going to be very simple for you to check the box and mark this first building block of governance as complete. If you don't already have this done, this is an effort that could take a very long time.

Establishing the process and rolling it out by focusing first on the regulatory requirements of your industry is the perfect first step because everyone can understand the need to ensure that your company, as a whole, is compliant. Follow that with policies about processes that add business value, as defined in a Value Stream Map or exercise. And finally, any other process that is tackled initially should be either aligned to a policy or eliminated as non-valuable. DLPs should also have the applicable policy number(s) documented such that if a business process is to be changed, the supporting policy is first referenced.

Reference Documentation

All industries have terminology that is specific to its way of doing business. Hearing the word "amortization" will immediately clue you in that we are talking about loans. Many industries use common words in very specific ways, such as the word "provider." In healthcare, a provider is a person or organization that offers services to patients. In social services, a provider is someone to gives something that is needed, such as a food bank as a provider of food to the needy. In some industries provider and supplier may be used interchangeably. The point is, it is important to understand the terminology used by your organization or industry and to ensure that common definitions are used.

There are many places to find data definitions. Try these spots to find terminology and definitions in your organization - look for "Glossary," "Dictionary," "Vocabulary," or "Terms":

- Company intranet sites
- SharePoint sites
- Databases
- Systems
- Code Map documents
- Policies and rules about terminology

It may seem strange, but very few companies have a common set of terminologies across the entire organization. The main reasons to have common terms is to make communication and reporting easier between parties and ensure that data is consistent to make better decisions. Having common terms is far less common than you would expect. Let me give you an example.

The term "Active" is pretty universal across all industries. In general, when you think of the term "Active" it means that the relationship with the entity is currently in place. Following are some examples of where it exists across different entities: at a bank it is applicable for accounts and clients; at an insurance company it is applicable for members, providers, employer groups, and brokers; at a manufacturing company it is applicable for accounts, product lines or products, and distributors.

How do you define "Active?" Is it the presence of a contract with an effective date before today and termination date in the future? Is it anyone who has placed an order within 30 days? Is it someone who has money in their account over the last quarter?

You can see that the simple term "Active" could have many definitions between industries, or even between departments. Hence the need to establish common vocabulary and more descriptive terminology.

Let me give you another example. Walk into any restaurant or fast food place and order "a hamburger." Without the context of where you are geographically or what restaurant chain you are in, you may have very different expectations than you will experience with the delivered food. In general, most Americans will expect a bun, a patty of beef, and some variety of condiments – usually ketchup and mustard. But if you are in Utah, it may come with "fry sauce." In England, that burger might come with a fried egg. In Japan, it may be a mushroom patty instead of beef. Will it have pickles, lettuce, tomato, onion, sauerkraut, mayonnaise, or cheese? As you can see from this simple example, vocabulary is very important.

If you don't have a corporate glossary or vocabulary already stored, it is still very likely a quick win. Computer systems are a common place to find vocabulary; it is present in virtually every database that has a data model. To establish a database, a data model must be built. And to populate the data model, a data dictionary is required. Even if the database is home grown, it likely has a data dictionary.

Ask your technical people who maintain and administer the database to extract and provide you with the data dictionary. Chances are you will end up with a collection of them that have common terms but the definitions don't align. This is where you can establish your first enterprise governance artifact – an Enterprise Glossary (Glossary for short).

The *Glossary* will contain all the terms and their definitions used throughout your company. Note: when requesting the data dictionaries, make sure that table or field attribute names are included. You will be shocked at how many "Effective Dates" you'll have on the list. If you don't know what attribute and/or table it comes from, it is a pretty meaningless data element. Request that it be specifically descriptive such as "Network Effective Date" or "Address Effective Date."

Once you have collected all of the Glossaries, it is important to ensure that they align with system *data dictionaries*. Ensure that there is a column that tells you what source/system the dictionary came from. It is also a good idea to have a column that identifies the business unit that maintains or creates the information for each system, table or attribute, as applicable.

Combine them into a single document and sort by name. Identify how many terms are repeated. Also find synonyms or known words that are used synonymously in your organization and put them all together.

With your consolidated list in hand, bring together the business units responsible for Creating or Modifying information.

- Host discussions and align on common meanings for the terms.

- If the definition really is different, agree to add descriptors, like the ones in the Effective Date example.
- The objective is to arrive at common names for the same meaning and common meaning for the same names.
- Whenever possible, avoid letting the root of a word reside in the definition. An example of what not to do: Member: someone who is a member of a group. A better definition would be: Member: a person who is part of a designated program or group.
- Check your definitions with the group of people designated as consumers of the data to ensure that the terms and definitions make sense throughout the lifecycle of the information.

Once you have compiled your Enterprise Glossary and received approval by the business users, your technical partners need to accept the definitions and update the data dictionaries. This group usually includes the database administrators and/or IT application development, architecture or engineers. If they don't work with you to establish the common data dictionaries, you haven't really solved the problem.

A system may also have a set of *reference data* or values, such as a list of states or countries. When a user is in the User Interface, reference values are the choices in drop-down lists. In a database, these live on a specific reference data table and may also be maintained on an external document. Reference data is different from the Glossary because it is the detailed values available for each defined term. You may define country as "an independently governed group of people in a defined geographic area that is recognized as an Independent State or Country by the international community." Your definition would not include a list of countries. Yet you will have a list of recognized countries that are the specific reference values allowed to be applied in your systems.

A step beyond the reference values is a document commonly called a *Code Map*. Code Map documents take the data dictionary and Glossary terms and collect the reference values. Databases generally store numeric, alphabetical or alphanumeric codes that align to human readable values. Hence, each country has a country code in each system. That country code may not be the same in each system.

The Code Map document collects all the specific codes and ties them to a Master corporate standard for country codes. Many organizations utilize the International Organization for Standardization (ISO) codes as their Master codes, and I highly recommend that as a success strategy. Some organizations established their Code Maps on their original or "legacy" system values, which they may or may not still use.

A best practice is to align codes to industry or international standards. The great benefit of doing so is to allow for easy mapping when in an interoperability situation. This is true whether it is an internal integration, business process hand-off, or connecting with information from an external third party.

The Code Map should align with the Enterprise Glossary and provide the alphanumeric codes that literally map the values from one system or another to the central designation. This is a lot of detail work, but it is a big win that can be accomplished in a relatively short time period.

The wins and artifacts described up to this point of this chapter rely on tight collaboration between you/your representative, business resources and Information Technology/Information Systems (IT/IS) professionals. The next few topics are very IT/IS-centric. The topics are Enterprise Information Model, Data Models, and Enterprise Logical Data Model. If you are a business, rather than IT/IS, professional, this may be a bit technical. If you work with Data Models regularly, this will be a very brief overview.

The idea of an Enterprise Information Model (EIM) is to visually describe how information flows across the company throughout its life-cycle. This artifact is 100% dependent on having a common Enterprise Glossary. The EIM puts business terms into relational models. A relational model groups like topics together on a table and puts attribute information that describes the topic on each table. An example of this is an Address Table. Most of us know that an address will have a house or building number, street name, suite or apartment, if applicable, a city name, state name, and zip code. A country code may also be included. And a county code is usually implied, although not always specified. See *Figure 4* for an illustration of the different views in the physical model and the logical model.

Figure 4 – Comparing Physical and Logical Database tables

mem_addr	Member Address
addr1	Address line 1
addr2	Address line 2
city_code	City
cnty_code	County
st_code	State
zip_code	Zip Code
cntry_code	Country
addr_start_dt	Address Start Date
addr_end_dt	Address End Date
Physical data model	*Logical data model*

End Figure 4

Logical Models are written in business language. Physical Models are written in technical language. If you have ever seen a data model, you would expect each table to look similar to the example in *Figure 4*. You see the table name at the top and the specific attributes listed below. In general, each table represents a single topic or idea. Some attributes on the Logical model will not appear on the Physical model. These usually represent custom created or defined User Defined Attributes (UDA). UDA's almost always live on a separate table, but may be modeled for the business on the Logical table where they make the most sense. The Physical model would not include them on the table. Physical model also include "keys" that point to where the information may be found, i.e. sk = source key, fk = foreign key, nk = natural key, etc.

In a data model, the relationship between each table is shown by connector lines with arrows or symbols that represent one-way, two-way, and/or one-to-one, or one-to-many relationships. Each table in each system or database is unique to that system.

An Address table for Members may exist in a claims payment system or in a library card management system. Having the same or similar names does not equate to common tables (and it's why the Enterprise Glossary is so important). *Figure 5* illustrates a simplistic data model.

Figure 5 – Simple Data Model illustration

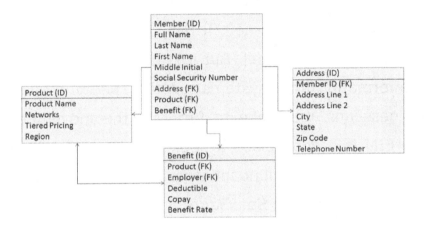

End Figure 5

An Enterprise Information Model (EIM) does not generally list the attributes, such as Address Line 1 or Region (from the above model); the attributes are shown on the Enterprise Logical Data Model. The EIM groups like topics together and shows the relationship of the ideas across the organization, not specifically tied to a single system or database.

The EIM is important because it helps illustrate the flow of information from system to system and business unit to business unit. A well-defined and modeled EIM is a high-level, logical view of how information interacts across the life-cycle. It can illustrate where processes are broken or information is dropped on the journey. It has similar benefits to a business process model. But it is focused on the flow of information from systems not the specific steps a business unit may take to facilitate the movement. The EIM is a good place to look for efficiencies such as integration or redundant stores of information that could be eliminated. See *Figure 6* for a sample EIM.

Figure 6 – Enterprise Information Model sample

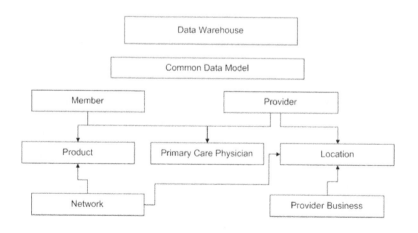

End Figure 6

A Business Process Model (BPM), on the other hand covers the specific steps taken by a business unit in the process of creating, maintaining, or consuming information.

A BPM generally shows each step of a process. Decision points are represented by diamond shapes. A "Yes" answer will take the process on one path and a "No" answer will divert to a different path.

Each group is represented by a swim lane. Notice in the example (*see Figure 7*) that the Host/Hostess is the first lane, the Server is the next lane, and so on. The process to service a customer at a restaurant requires six parties to participate – four people and two systems. Notice how the workflow moves from group to group.

In the model, you can clearly see the steps required by each party. This can assist you in determining the right staffing ratios as well as provide a view to evaluate and potentially eliminate any extra steps. A Bartender can service many more customers than a Waiter because they only have one step per order, whereas the Waiter has ten steps.

Figure 7 – Business Process Model

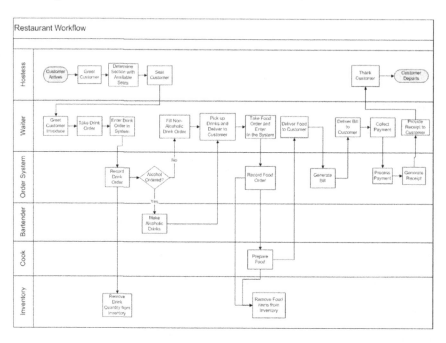

End Figure 7

Individual business process models can also be combined into a more complex view of business activities such as the Business Integration model shown in *Figure 8.* Within this kind of model, you begin to see how business process models, data models, systems, requirements and infrastructure

114

begin to support one another to enable the seamless flow of information.

The restaurant model we saw in *Figure 7*, requires a computer system to hold the orders, pass the information to the cook, and ultimately provide billing and payment capabilities.

To accomplish these items in a seamless way, each business process must interact with data, such as the menu for entering the order and the inventory management system that keeps track of the ingredients needed for each recipe. That in turn helps the manager set the price of items based on the replacement price of the ingredients. The employee time is logged into yet another database and that provides the information to generate paychecks.

The model in *Figure 8* was not developed specific to a restaurant's business process, but you can apply the same integration model structure to illustrate how models work together. The business process follows the process steps and has specific terminology. The ordering system and inventory

management system have data models and a
database.

Figure 8 – Business Model Integration

Business Model Integration

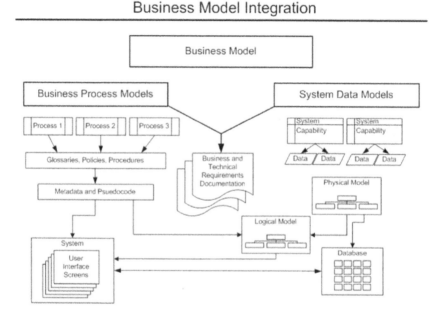

End Figure 8

You may be asking, "What do these operational
and data models have to do with Data Governance?"

The day to day business of your company
follows a business process model, regardless of
whether your company is a mom-and-pop diner or an

international bank. If you don't know what steps are taken and what systems are used to support those business processes, chances are good that you have waste in your organization.

Creating business process models is something that can be done on a whiteboard or using sticky-notes on a wall. It is a low-cost method of modeling and eliminating waste. If you could save 1% of your employee's time, would you invest in that? That seems like a very achievable goal simply by eliminating a single step from everyone's process. What if your employee budget/cost is $10 Million per year? You just saved $100,000 per year. No small change for spending a little time modeling the team's workflow and finding the one step that is wasteful or unnecessary.

There are a lot of resources for business process modeling. This book is not dedicated to that subject. I merely want to highlight that governing your processes improves your bottom line and gives you information that is useful when making strategic decisions and planning roadmaps.

Chapter 4 Small Business Corner

Quick Wins: Look for best practices across your business. Give people credit and recognition for the great things they are already doing. This will increase buy-in.

Policies: Deciding how policies will be structured, maintained, and monitored early in your business will avoid many of the pitfalls that grow like weeds if not carefully tended. Taking the time early to be purposeful will eliminate redundancies and ensure consistent operations.

Glossaries, Data Dictionaries, and System Reference data: Establishing the culture that new vernacular must be documented, including new acronyms, and providing a place for that to occur will eliminate the very common problem in large organizations of having many different names for essentially the same thing.

Establish your Code Map early. Assume that at some point your business will need to interact with other businesses. Determine the right "industry standard" or international standard set of codes and use them from the beginning.

The section on Enterprise Information Model, Data Models, and Enterprise Logical Data Model may not seem applicable to your business at this stage. However, if you will assign someone to learn about them and begin a map of your data flows (the Enterprise Information Model) in an easy format like PrimaryScape™ (see Chapter 6, page 160, *Figure 9*), you will have a clear graphical visual of how information flows from one business function to the next, which will set you up to implement a more advanced model later.

Chapter 5 – Program Structure

"You can design and create, and build
the most wonderful place in the world.
But it takes people to make the dream a reality."
Walt Disney

Now that you have a better idea of what you already have, it is time to decide how to structure your governance organization. The decisions made will have a big impact on the success of your undertaking. That does not mean that there is only one right way. It does mean that you should try to pick the method that will work best in your organization.

Two main methods exist for implementing a data governance program: Top-Down or Bottom-Up. In a Top-Down model, the executive leaders make decisions and pass them down to the data stewards for implementation. And in a Bottom-Up model, as expected from the name, the work is driven as more of a grass roots endeavor where the data stewards self-direct and report up to the executive level. Both models have merit and can be successful. They can also coexist provided the boundaries, expectations, and process flow are agreed to in advance. Which model your company chooses will be largely determined by the culture of the company and your leadership model.

The Top-Down model is best suited to companies with strong leaders and a very clear executive-driven strategy and/or mission. Leaders who are deeply invested in the organization's activities will be in a good position to drive decisions and set the direction of a data governance program. Either model requires executive buy-in to accomplish the objectives. The Top-Down model puts the accountability squarely on the shoulders of the leadership of the organization. Let's examine the Pros and Cons.

Pros	Cons
• Governance strategies will align naturally to	• Executives tend to take a 70,000-foot view of the

company initiatives • Any necessary funding will be understood and more easily obtained • Questions of authority will rarely arise as directives will be from the Top • Implementation will be faster because the program will be supported by the strategic goals	activities of the company. • Decisions made by executives may not align with the realities of the day to day capabilities. In short, their expectations may not be fully realized within the structure, timeline, or funding that is allocated. • Only the most strategic components of the necessary work will be of interest to executives. Much of the foundational work that must be accomplished will be delegated and the level of effort may not be well understood.

While these Pros and Cons are only a quick peek at the full list, they do present the stance that Top-Down implementation will have many benefits.

Bottom-Up implementation strategies are often driven by a person or group who is passionate about improvements and change. These initiatives may be best suited for implementation within a single business unit rather than across a larger enterprise. It will also require executive sponsorship, but may not fall under the same level of executive scrutiny.

Pros	Cons
• The people leading the implementation are at the level where the work needs to be performed. • Small, quick wins can be accomplished operationally without significant overhead, investment, or structure	• Any necessary funding may be more difficult to get allocated • Executives may not appreciate the value of the work being done • Organizational structure may not support the activities that are needed and that may limit the scope

• *The points of focus can vary depending on the needs of each data steward's team* • *Timelines are looser and self-imposed*	• *Enterprise Architecture may not be fully aligned with the needs of the business* • *Culture may play a bigger factor in the success or failure* • *It may be difficult to overcome "blockers" without leadership authority*

Both models are perfectly viable. Which one you choose will depend on many factors, most importantly the method should align to the expected outcomes. As part of the chartering process for your program to implement a governance organization, you should already have a good idea of the expected scope and structure and already be aligned with your supporting leadership team.

Define the roles

The first step of any implementation is to define the roles. Generally, the roles in a governance organization include a Steering Committee, some

Data Stewards, and Data Custodians. These three groups are the minimum necessary roles for success. It should be noted that one person may play more than a single role, but they should understand the differences.

Steering Committee

The Steering Committee members provide oversight and approvals. The members should have the appropriate authority to make decisions for the company (or business unit). For either Top-Down or Bottom-Up models, the Steering Committee reviews the decisions or recommendations of the data stewards, discusses them related to the strategic objectives for which they are accountable, and provides authoritative decisions. In a Top-Down model, they may also set the strategy.

The Steering Committee should meet frequently enough that their oversight remains relevant. For a stable governance organization, quarterly meetings may be appropriate. For a newly formed governance organization, meetings should be at least monthly, if not twice per month in order to support the momentum that you are trying to build. You, as the Driver of the implementation, should present the status of the implementation in the same way that a project manager reports their status. This is usually done weekly, even if there is not a scheduled meeting. Keeping this group informed and engaged is one of your primary objectives and will be the key to your success. The members of the Steering Committee should represent the leadership structure of the governed organization. They should, generally, include the senior leader of each major business division, each IT function, Finance, and Human Resources. For many organizations, this is the C-Suite. For some organizations, the Senior or Executive Vice Presidents may fill these seats. It is important that all functional areas of the governed organization are included.

The Steering Committee plays one additional critical role – the Data Stewards should be accountable to them, preferably via an employment structure, although dotted-line or matrixed organizations can work provided the matrixed structure is a company norm. Having the Data

Stewards directly accountable to the Steering Committee members ensures significantly better outcomes. Stewards whose boss puts the success of governance in their goals are more invested in successful outcomes.

Data Owner

Complex or Matrixed organizations will often have a leadership role between the Steering Committee and the Data Stewards. This is the Data Owner. The Data Owner is specifically accountable for an entire data Domain, and only one. This is a particularly useful strategy if the data Domain crosses business units or divisions.

For example, in healthcare you may find that provider credentialing falls into a Quality division while provider enrollment falls into a Production/Operation Services division. But both create and manage "provider" data. In this case, the Data Owner of the Provider Domain would be accountable to two members of the Steering Committee. The Data Stewards may be assigned form either or both divisions; I recommend having one from each.

Data Stewards are accountable to the Data Owners. This structure is usually unnecessary in smaller organizations or localized business unit governance.

Data Stewards

The Data Steward is the role that has the most direct oversight and control of the data governance in any organization. There is a phrase that "every employee is a data steward." This is true to a point. Yes, everyone should pay attention to the information and data that they handle and "care" for it. But the role of Data Steward is very specific to the parties who will review and recommend approval of governance artifacts, such as policies or terminology, and they will interact with the stakeholders that they represent.

Data Stewards should have an allotted amount of time for governance activities cleared by their direct management. They should meet at least weekly. Their primary function is to be the eyes, hands, and feet of the governance organization. They will meet with subject matter experts, data custodians, and other people who "do" the work and ensure that policies are understood and enforced, processes are documented, data quality is monitored, measured and improved, and they will have an important part to play in change management.

Stakeholders

A stakeholder is a party who has an interest in or is affected by an activity or change. While it may be a nice idea to think that everyone who has an interest in how information is created, managed or consumed would be a data steward, the reality is that most of them must be represented by a smaller subset of individuals. The Data Stewards, then, have accountability up to the Data Owner or Steering Committee as well as down to the stakeholders.

Data Quality and "Fix-it" Analysts

Two other roles are important: Data Quality analysts and "Fix-It" analysts. The Data Quality analysts are specifically charged with the measurement and continuous improvement of the quality or health of the data used in the organization.

They perform the root cause analysis on data issues and either submit incident tickets to IT requesting incident resolution or a change request for a modification or in the system causing the data inconsistency. They would also open work items, or tasks, for the people charged with putting hands on keyboards to fix the data, also known as "Fix-It" analysts/processors. We devote an entire exciting chapter on Data and Information Quality later. These roles will be covered in more detail.

Data Custodians and Architects

On the Information Technology side of the house, there are two primary roles that interface with the governance organization: Data Custodians and Data/Information Architects or Modelers. Data Custodians have the accountability for the systems where data or information is maintained or used. They may have job titles like VP of Application Development or Director of Data Warehousing. Some organizations give the Data Custodian role to a level closer to the Data Stewards – people with close interactions with the systems but with varying levels of separation. A Manager of Systems and Infrastructure or an Enterprise Information or Business Architect might be named a Data Custodian. Essentially these are the people with the authority to make decisions about the maintenance, improvement, and/or management of technology systems or applications. They are a critical support role to ensure that decisions made about the organization's information can be supported within the systems that house it.

Like the Data Owners and Stewards on the business side of the organization, the Data Custodians should also be accountable to the Steering Committee and have regular interactions with the Data Stewards.

Enterprise Architects and Data Modelers have an important role to play in data governance. Typically, they are accountable for the design and documentation of technology capabilities for the company with the associated applications, data models, and integrations. They assist with keeping the business strategy aligned with the appropriate security and technology supporting infrastructure. In an organization with robust, mature governance, the architects or data modelers may have the accountability to manage or maintain data lineage tools, information catalogs, data lakes, and other data assets to support the tactical and strategic needs of the business.

Data Lineage

Data lineage is much like a family lineage. It describes the origins, modifications, movement, translations/transformations, and type of data. Few organizations implement true data lineage without a tool. The relational nature of data makes traceability extremely complex, especially when data with similar terms and/or definitions is combined into a single data store, such as a Data Lake, Enterprise Data Warehouse, or other "Big Data" solution.

The Data Lineage tool provides a map to find the upstream and downstream disposition of the information in question. Data lineage tools provide the key to who created the data, how it is changed, by whom, what the data means, where is it accessed and how it is related to other terms; it stitches data together into a fabric titled, "Business Information."

Data lineage is made up of a few key components:

- Documentation of where data originates
- Documentation of how it is created and managed
- What the data means
- Classification, Labels, or other organization techniques
- Who uses it
- Rules about the data
- What systems it is housed in
- What processes transform it
- How it relates to other information in the business

There are benefits to data lineage in a governance program. The primary benefit is an understanding of who creates and who manages the specific data in the organization. This is extremely helpful if you are a consumer of the information and you question the validity or accuracy of information that has made a journey to get to you. Often an enterprise platform will include a Master Data Management (MDM) component. The data lineage tool helps ensure that the transformation happens as expected.

Compliance is an important benefit of data lineage. Most audits look for the integrity of the data, an understanding of how it is used (things like desk level procedures, segregation of duties or security/access controls), and adherence to specific standards. The data lineage tool provides a level of trust in the data by clearly showing how that data arrived in the system, process, or report.

It is a great tool for root cause analysis and data quality. Since a data lineage tool will show the origins, movement, transformations, combinations, and interpretations of the data through an organization's processes and systems, the data analyst can reference it for the end-to-end lifecycle of the data.

Chapter 5 Small Business Corner

The small business is most likely going to use the Top-Down model. You will still be very connected to all levels of your business and are likely to be directing the activities and culture of your company. As your company grows, you will need to decide the right time to put a governance program structure into place.

The most important thing you can do is to stress the fact that *every employee is a steward of company data.* If you can get this into your culture early, adoption and structure will be easier when you're ready to formalize a program.

Chapter 6 – The Operating Model

"Design is not just what it looks like and feels like.
Design is how it works."
Steve Jobs

We have talked about Why data governance is important; What data governance is; and How to set up a program that will be a success. Now it is time to get a bit more detailed about the unique structures within the program. The term operating model is used to describe the people, processes and technology that will be needed for success. It includes everyone from the executive leadership to the people with hands-on-keyboards needed to make the changes in the data and every step in between. Every one of those roles and responsibilities that we spoke of in the previous chapter will have a part in the operating model.

People

The Executive Steering Committee

The executive steering committee has the accountability to set strategy and direction for the Data Stewards to follow. Ideally your steering committee is made up of those people who set the strategic direction and make decisions to guide the company. It is very important for the two to align. Whether you set up a Top-Down or Bottom-Up organization, the steering committee is the body that should have the final say and approval on policies and initiatives undertaken by the governance organization. This body should review and approve the initial governance charter and champion the initiatives that will make it a success.

The steering committee should meet at least monthly. These meetings should include a status report from each major initiative and a review of the data quality activities of each Domain. It is the steering committee who would approve any funding requests. And they should be strong champions, especially in a voluntary model of organization.

Significant projects that will impact data should, in addition to the usual project approval process, be brought to the steering committee for review and prioritization. Through this additional level of oversight, the steering committee ensures that the governance needs of the organization are met and projects that may not have a strong business case if undertaken by a single business unit could be given more weight if they will benefit the governance process in general or set up a pilot process or technology for a governance initiative.

It is important that the executive steering committee is a strong voice in the change management process. A strategic move is to make yourself available to them for private conversations. Don't assume that it is the case, but you may find that some of your leadership simply does not understand the principles of data governance or the benefits that will be reaped. That's okay; you have been there; we all have. Give them the opportunity to meet with you individually to discuss the impacts to their data Domains. This seemingly small step will buy you social capital with the leadership group. It allows them to save face by not having to admit that they don't know much about data governance, and it helps personalize the process for the business units for which they are responsible.

Getting this executive-level buy in early is critical. Once the program has rolled down a level or two, additional levels of resistance will be uncovered. It will be important to have educated and engaged executive leaders who can help soften resistance within their organization.

Especially at this point in the conversation, it's critical that you follow the principles of change management. You must help people understand what governance is and why it is good for the company. Everyone, including you, will need to go through the Change Continuum. (*See additional information about Change Management in the References and on my website at www.getgoverned.com*).

Everyone goes through the phases of Awareness, Understanding, Acceptance and finally, Commitment. If you can go through these phases quickly, you will be able to help others go through these phases. It is particularly important for the Data Stewards to get to the Commitment phase as quickly as possible. Of course, everyone handles change differently, but if you exude confidence and assurance, the negative impacts will be minimized and the benefits maximized.

The Data Stewards Council

The Data Steward is the core of data governance. Each Data Domain will need to identify their data stewards. It is often said that everybody in the company is a data steward. The statement contains a lot of truth. Anybody who uses, maintains, creates, manages, enforces compliance or works in a system that holds information has an accountability to be a good steward.

We live in an increasingly complex world, and there are increasing pressures and real-life problems like data piracy, corporate espionage, and other threats to the privacy and protection of our information and data. It is more important than ever for every person in the organization to be a good steward of the data to ensure that there following the right policies and the right security protocols. Nurturing a sense of care for data; helping the stewards understand what is protected what is not protected and to what industry regulations you are accountable will support the collaborative spirit of the Data Stewards. Everybody really is a steward, and that is a fundamental thing to help your people understand.

As you begin to evangelize about data governance, one of the most difficult things you will encounter is instilling that sense of care and accountability in people and groups within the company who aren't specifically assigned to a role called, "data steward," "data owner," or "data custodian." These people are an important foundation of success. Whether you call them Subject Matter Experts (SMEs) or Stakeholders, they need to be involved from the beginning.

The Data Stewards and the Data Steward Council are the cogs that turn data governance. It is within the structure and members of the Stewards

Council that governance happens. The data stewards will meet regularly; I recommend that they meet at least weekly.

The primary reason that funding will be needed for the data governance organization is because Data Steward should be an actual job title have a dedicated job description. The data steward job should be full-time, if possible. If it is not possible to fund someone with full-time employment, at least a significant part, up to 50%, of the Steward's job responsibilities should be dedicated to governance. There is a lot of work that goes into putting a successful governance organization into production and maintaining it over time. It is not something that happens accidentally. It is not something that will be done off the side of someone's desk. And it will not have the proper attention if the data stewards don't have stewardship as part of their job description.

The role that funding plays is to ensure that the steering committee or the business units sponsoring data governance have provided adequate resources and support to do the work needed for proper governance.

The Stewards Council is the group of people who come together to set policies, identify data management practices, and to ensure that the data and information assets of the company are cared for – stewarded and managed. For the Council to be effective, at least weekly meetings are necessary. It is likely that more than two meetings in a week will be required during the set-up phase.

In an organization that I worked at recently, the data stewards Council met twice a month. But there were workgroups that came together several times per week. As each specific initiative is undertaken, especially in the early days of the governance program or in immature governance organizations, workgroups need to be established to accomplish the specific tasks and make the decisions to achieve the desired outcome.

Let me give you an example. One of the big buzz-words in business today is "Data Lake." A data lake is simply a collection of information on the same topic, or in our context, in the same Domain. Some organizations create non-specific data lakes, which simply collect all information. Generally, information in a data lake may be structured and unstructured. (Recall that structured data comes from a database and unstructured data would be something like an Excel spreadsheet.) Once a data lake is put into production initially, and people begin to use it, they will begin to understand that there are things missing. This is normal. It is not a reflection on the people who implement the data lakes; it reflects the lack of understanding of everyone who provided requirements. Most of us have never worked with a data lake before. Inevitably, there will be a series of change requests that need to be submitted. These are going to come from all over the company and they are going to be competing for a finite set of resources to fulfill the change requests.

In order to ensure that the most critical things for the company, in general, are completed first, you will need to establish some type of rating or ranking system. This system will require that the data stewards come up with criteria for what's most important for your company. Is it important to you that a customer facing issue is resolved before an employee facing issue? Is it important to you that a data quality item is address before or after a transactional issue is identified? Those types of questions need to be asked and answered by the data stewards.

The stewards will need to come up with the criteria that is machine readable. Gray matter, or the human brain, can make a subjective decision whereas silicon matter, a computer, can only sort and prioritize using mathematical algorithms. You simply can't have people making every one of these decisions, primarily because there isn't enough bandwidth; nobody can afford to pay for that level of staffing. Unless machine readable algorithms can be established, the stewards would need to meet and review every single request manually.

There will be many things of this nature that will need to be established by the steward council. Things such as resolution of data issues, setting up data lineage systems, and especially data quality will be given to the caring hands of the stewards to establish and/or resolve.

To establish the Stewards Council, the Data Owners of each Domain should appoint no more than two stewards to represent the interests of the entire business unit. The stewards should review and have input on the finalized Charter document. And they should be given training on how to enact their duties as stewards. They will, likely, need a crash course on data governance. A consulting firm could be utilized to provide this training or you could do it yourself, if you are comfortable enough with these topics.

Once the data stewards' council is established, you will need to decide on the most important items to tackle first. Ideally this direction would come from the Steering Committee, but the Stewards may also decide on the topics that are most pressing. If you have already identified your set of important ranking criteria, you would apply it to the list of initiatives you want to tackle.

As mentioned before, being a data steward is a significant time commitment. To help manage the time allocation, a regular schedule of meetings and subgroups should be established. The supervisors of each data steward will need allow enough time for effective representation of the business unit. As the champion of the governance program, it may fall to you and/or the Executive Sponsor to help justify and clear the path for steward participation.

Basic change management applies here. I have included a resource to help you with the change management process in the References section of this book or it is downloadable from my website at www.getgoverned.com/change_management. You need to master change management to implement data governance effectively within your organization.

Change management will be an important part of establishing and maintaining momentum with Steward Council. The Steward Council should submit regular status reports to the Steering Committee, just like any project. They should be accountable to the data owners or the steering committee directly and they will interface with the data custodians on a regular basis.

As a data steward, you should have a very good relationship with the data custodian, the data modeler, and/or the enterprise architect as well as the person who manages the Code Map for your company. This group of people help make the decisions on what information assets are exposed to the Stewards and have a say in how they are governed. The data stewards have the business accountability and the data custodians have the IT or infrastructure accountability. These two roles go together and neither can be successful without the other. It's important that you have a shared vision. It's important that you have the same priorities. You only have those things if you have regular and constant communication.

With the Steward Council stood up and your objectives identified you have the beginning of a structure and organization that will prove successful.

Data Quality Analysts and Fix-It Analysts

The Data Stewards will set policies and establish initiatives. But you need to have people who can do the work. I suggest two different skill levels of analysts. The first is a Data Quality analyst. This level of person is skilled in doing root cause analysis, understanding cause and effect, and may be a Six Sigma Green Belt. Some companies give this level of analyst the rights to configure systems and even use SQL to update reference data. The second skill level is the "Fix-it" analysts. These analysts will take direction from the data stewards and the data quality analysts and will actually work in the user interfaces of systems to correct faulty information, conduct validation activities, and perform general documentation activities.

Now you have an end-to-end program from identifying a strategy to developing a policy to implementing the system to giving a business process life and to managing and maintaining both the system and the process together hand in hand to ensure that it follows this the standards and the objectives of the governance organization.

Process

Data Asset Management

The natural next topic is data asset management. Data asset management is an important component of data governance. Data, or information, is a strategic asset. What do we mean by a strategic asset? It means that information is money. Information provides the framework and the tools to make informed decisions about strategy, investments, direction, threats, opportunities, and all the other aspects of doing business on a day-to-day basis. Particularly for the leadership of the company, information as a data asset is critical.

Data asset management includes quite a few components including systems, business process models, and governance structure that we've talked about. But there are specific things that we've mentioned above that impact data asset management. Primary among them is the Code Map. Stating that the codes should be based on industry standards isn't quite enough. A Code Map document is a method of aligning all the terminology and codes.

Because systems use codes, not descriptions, to point to and represent information, it is important to note that each code across the enterprise and across systems may be different for the same information.

For example, for an insurance company you may have information about doctors in the claims system, in a provider data management system, and in the credentialing system. They will all have some data elements in common. One of the sets of information that they will have in common is a list of states. The United States of America has 50 states and several protectorates such as Puerto Rico, US Virgin Islands and Guam. Each of those geographic areas has a code. The International Organization for Standardization (ISO) has assigned a two-digit code to each of those areas. Countries also have a two-digit code assigned to them by the ISO. The United States is US, Canada is CA, Columbia is CO. You get the idea.

The concept of a Code Map is that it takes the different codes which are represented in each individual application and maps the codes to the descriptions found in the technology solution or system. And it should align those codes to a standardized list.

Hence, if one system, say the claims system, makes use of the alpha codes for states and the provider data management system uses a numeric code for states assigned alphabetically beginning with 01 and ending with 99, the code map would align the values from both systems to the standardized set.

I would always recommend the use of industry standard codes for your company master code set or "conform code." If the industry standard for ISO is a two-digit alpha code, but your provider data management system uses numeric codes, such as "79" for the United States, the Code Map would cross reference the code "79" with the description "United States of America" to the alpha code "US" in the Code Map. If your claim system uses "US" as the alpha code for the United States the Code Map would say the claims code "US" with description "United States" aligns to Code Map conform code "US." In this manner, you can take data from more than one system and more than one way of describing it and align it to a central set of values.

Sample Code Map

System	Code	Description	Conform Code
Claims	US	United States	US
Provider Data Management	79	United States of America	US

The primary value that the Code Map provides is in building integrations between your company and third parties' systems. Most companies these days are not stand-alone companies. We all use a variety of vendors, third parties, and outside labor to do work for us or partner with us to accomplish our goals. Face it, we live in a global society; with new regulations, such as Europe's General Data Protection Regulation (GDPR), having standard values and codes is more important than ever. The Code Map and its alignment to international standards makes the interaction and interoperability between systems and companies, such as vendors or third parties, possible.

Technology

The advent of Big Data, Cloud Computing and Data Lakes has provided an opportunity for new tools and technologies. A data lineage tools is an important method of keeping track of information. Data lineage means the ability to trace data or information from its inception, where it's created in your organization, through every transformation, combination with other piece of data, maintenance, and consumption throughout the lifecycle of that piece of information.

Think of data lineage like family genealogies or ancestry research. If I want to know where I'm from, I can ask where my parents are from. My parents are from a small town in central Utah. Their parents also are from the same small town. But both sets of their paternal grandparents migrated to the United States from Scandinavia – Denmark on my Father's side and Sweden on my Mother's side. My father's maternal grandmother is descended from a long line of Dutch emigrants that came across on the Mayflower. My mother's maternal grandparents have been in the United States since just before the Revolutionary war when they migrated to the United States from England. So, my genealogy, my ancestry, or lineage, is northern European and generally Scandinavian.

Data lineage is essentially the same thing. Where did this information originate? Who maintains it? How has it transformed or combined? What team, system or organization has a hand in the way this information is managed, where it goes and how it ends up? A data lineage tool provides a map. It provides information such as the class of data: reference data, transactional data, or demographic data. The specific classes can be set up by every company to meet their needs. What category or domain of data is it?

In our healthcare example, the tool might identify a term as part of the Claim domain or it might also be a part of the Member domain. If this data originated in the member domain, it's very likely that it's going to have something to do with the medical care of the people who have paid their premiums to be covered by a health insurance plan.

As information is integrated and transformed, the data lineage tool provides the traceability of how the information is combined and flows through systems and processes. It can show when it transforms into something completely different. It is just like genealogies of people; it branches and splits and comes together and make something new. That's also how data lineage is, and you can see that without some type of tool to keep track of it or organize it, understanding where your data comes from and where it goes is incredibly complicated. In fact, the people who create the data may have absolutely no idea who uses it. And the people who use the data may have absolutely no idea who created it initially.

An example of this happened to me recently. I was working with a group of people who were about to lose the person identification number that they have used in their system for years to perform their process and keep track of data. They were losing it because we were shutting off the mainframe system that had been their primary source of the identifying information. The legacy identifier was being replaced by a different set of identifiers from another system. The people using that identifier out of their legacy system had no idea of the origin of the number. When I communicated to the entire company that this specific identifier was going to be retired, they didn't know that it would affect them. They never said, "I need help with the new ID." They only knew how to perform their business process with the number that an integration placed in their system. This is a good example of how easy it is to lose track of information. No organization is so simple that information is safe from transformation and loss of context.

If you want to use your data, and you want to leverage the rich information that you collected over the years you have been in business, you need to understand the full life-cycle of where your data comes from, where it's used, how it's combined, and how you can utilize it for other processes. Data lineage tools, Code Map and system schematics are very important.

By schematics, I don't necessarily mean the architecture of an individual application or system. I'm really talking about the interplay of one system to another. One of the tools that I used regularly when talking to business stakeholders who don't understand technical terms and don't understand the architectural and infrastructure components, is a system schematic drawing.

I use a simple to understand system that an amazing architect, Andreas Amundin, invented called PrimaryScape™. Using this very simple notation, I can describe how information flows from one system to another to a non-technical individual. This helps them understand how the information that they use may have originated far away from their business unit or their functional area.

It is hard to see in grayscale, but structures are represented by light blue boxes, yellow boxes within them are information, and behaviors are green octagons. Teams are teal boxes and have a stick figure icon. Arrows represent the transfer and direction and intent of information flow. (See it in color at www.getgoverned.com/primaryscape_model)

Figure 9 - PrimaryScape™ System Model

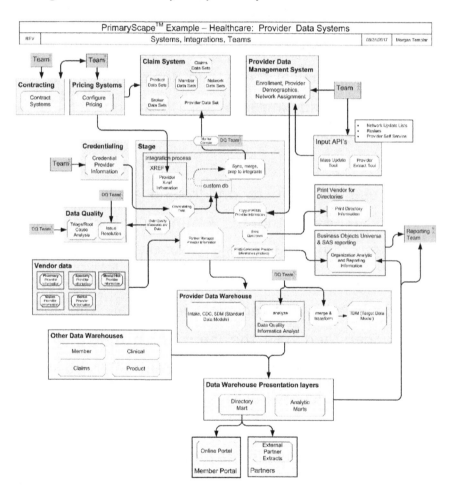

The image above is a model of a provider data management group's systems, teams, and data flows. It illustrates where information is modified by people (Teams) and where it moves via a technical integration. In this accessible visual, even non-technical team members can understand who/what is responsible to keep information flowing. And it allows leaders to identify potential waste in the flow and opportunities for strategic investment in automation or simplification.

End Figure 9

If I am accountable for a data strategy, I need to understand what data we use for our business. System schematics for my business unit not only includes the primary applications or systems that we use, it also includes unstructured data that is used on a regular basis by our team. I should take a moment and quickly explained the difference between structured data and unstructured data because I don't want to assume that you understand what that means.

Structured data is information that falls within a relational database such as Oracle™ or Netezza™. It has a data model with attributes and codes that point from table to table and represent the relationships and the affiliations between one set of attributes and another set of attributes. It is constrained to certain structures and highly normalized. It is usually what occurs in a physical data model and is the domain of information technology and information systems.

Unstructured data, or denormalized data, is what the business uses when they're using an Excel spreadsheet, an Access database or Word documents or tables.

Any information that the business uses, whether from a structured database or an unstructured source, should be included in a system schematic. If I don't know where my data is managed, maintained or created, I won't fully understand the information used to do business. Connecting structured and unstructured data is difficult and often discouraged by IT. But it may be necessary, especially for reporting or analytics. A system schematic or program schematic for a business unit should include both the structured and the unstructured data used within that organization.

Let's look at an example such a data validation exercise. I may take an extract of data out of the structured data system as a report. That report will be exported into Excel. Excel is now unstructured data. I use the Excel spreadsheet to make telephone calls to validate the information. I add a column so that the spreadsheet has a place to insert the information learned by making calls. If I'm told that the address has changed or the spelling of the name is different or that the person no longer works there, I need to record that information in the spreadsheet.

Performing data validation is generally undertaken for some kind of initiative or requirement – such as an accreditation standard or data quality initiative. When I complete this activity, and have collected the output, I will need to load the changes into my structured data set. There are many ways of doing that upload. You could have a system that does it for you, it can be scripted in, or can be typed in manually into user interface. I know where the data came from, and I have loaded it into my system. I have now used unstructured data as part of my structured data assets.

In this example, the system schematic would help me, as a data steward, understand the information that I have in my organization within my domain. I can explain how it is managed, if it is structured or unstructured, and how it is loaded into the system – either by manual entry or scripted in by some type of technical person or data custodian. This information helps me understand the root cause of data issues or where processes could be improved for greater efficiency. Data asset management includes the Code Map, data lineage tools, and system schematics. Data Policy Management is also part of data asset management.

The Enterprise Logical Data Model (ELDM) is like a business process model and an Enterprise Information Model. But it goes beyond either one to show all BPMs and all EIMs in a single consolidated view (*see Figure 10*). The ELDM is an artifact that you will only find in very mature governed organizations. The process to document, link, and model every business unit's process and system is an enormous undertaking. This is not a quick win. But it should be the long-term goal for a governed organization.

Figure 10 – Enterprise Logical Data Model

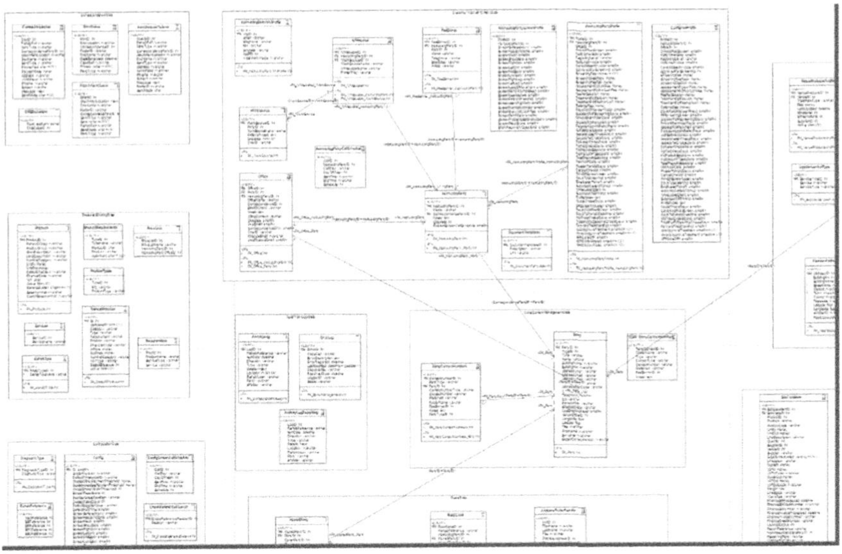

The image of this model is not intended for you to read. It is illustrative of the complexity of a true Enterprise-level logical data model.

Each row in each box represents either a piece of data, such as "Member Name" (recall the simple model of Figure 4 comparing physical and logical models on page 108) or it represents some kind of metadata such as the ID that represents the member in the database. That Member ID is a Foreign Key (FK), which points the analyst to the correct Member Record. As stated above, this is not a book on how to develop or read data models. But it is important to recognize that having a "map" of your data and how it connects is valuable and can help eliminate redundant business processes to maintain and gather necessary information.

End Figure 10

A Systems Inventory, like business process models, is a view of the specific systems and maps of how the computer systems we use for our business interactions. Some systems are stand alone and only have individual components and other systems are integrated using shared hardware and software components. A systems inventory is something that a business architect would construct and maintain. Because these vary significantly from company to company, I have not included an illustration.

As described in *Figure 10*, like an Enterprise Logical Data Model, a systems inventory can help avoid redundant information and inform where information flows across the company.

We have covered the different roles and the different uses of data asset management structures within your organization. It lays out a well-rounded program, from top to bottom – a steering committee, a data steward counsel, identified data custodians, and established data asset management, data policy and quality governance. The next chapter will cover the data quality program in detail.

Chapter 6 - Small Business Corner

The people, processes, and technologies described in this chapter are much more applicable to large complex organizations. While it may be helpful for your data stewards to be familiar with these concepts, most of them won't apply.

The Code Map will apply and should be utilized from the first day your company is in business! Keeping track of the meaning of information and consistently cross-referencing it to industry standard code sets will bring a level of maturity to the small business that will set it up for easier interoperability with vendors and other organizations.

Chapter 7 – Information Quality

"Quality is never an accident.
It is always the result of intelligent effort."
John Ruskin

A critical component of any governance program is information quality. Poor quality is often the catalyst for implementing a data governance program in the first place. The benefits of better quality data are sometimes difficult to quantify; however, it is so foundational that everyone can identify when it is insufficient.

How to set up an Information Quality Program

There are eight important steps in setting up an Information Quality program. These borrow heavily from the Six Sigma discipline (you will recognize the five-step Define, Measure, Analyze, Improve, and Control or "DMAIC" in these steps):

Step 1: Understand what is important to measure and where it resides

Step 2: Define the data rules – describe how to measure

Step 3: Analyze the data – what needs to improve

Step 4: Measure the data – Create Metrics

Step 5: Improve the data – implement clean up processes; add system edits

Step 6: Control the data – put a process in place to continually improve and manage the quality Metrics

Step 7: Report on the health of the data – Share results with your leadership team

Step 8: Repeat these steps for continuous improvement

A comprehensive data quality program includes many components beyond the quality assurance audit. It begins by identifying every time and place that data is created, moved, transformed, modified, and at rest sitting in a database or system. Think of this as Operational Data (typical quality assurance audits), Data on the Move, and Data at Rest.

By looking at information across the entire life-cycle, you can begin to see patterns and trends that may not be apparent in a one-dimensional audit.

Operational Data

The typical approach to quality assurance is to audit the work of processors, those people who enter data into a system. This one-dimensional approach has proven to be an ineffective method in today's complex technical environments. Attempting to audit 100% of transactions is extremely costly and generally only done for highly visible transactions such as setting financial rates or pricing. My experience has shown that across industries, most information that is managed is audited at a shockingly low rate of less than 10% of transactions. What that really means is that 90% of all information used to conduct business has not been checked for accuracy or compliant maintenance practices.

A better way to eliminate operational errors is to program "system edits" into the transaction system. These edits would prevent a processor from entering incorrect information at the source and can even provide checks for duplicate entry of data and other business rules. Recall our opening story. This kind of system edits would have prevented the nurse from ordering a medication with life-threatening consequences.

Both kinds of operational transactions should be measured and trended. They should be the basis for training programs and increased attention.

Data on the Move

Evaluating Data on the Move may be as simple as reading the logs as a system replicates a database, such as when an Oracle™ database is replicated using Golden Gate™. A database log file is generated that identifies any errors in the replication process and trends of information that does not move from system to system within the specified Service

Level Agreement (SLA) timeframe would be considered an error.

Beyond the simple log, when information is transformed using an Extract, Transform, Load (ETL) or Extract, Load, Transform (ELT), protocols can be written to monitor every single transaction for the applicable business rules and either hard stop the data transfer until the error is corrected or create an error report that can be worked after the fact as clean-up by the business users.

An example is setting data validation rules for addresses captured in a system. The address being passed from one system to the next must comply with US Postal Service standard formats. Any address that does not comply would be considered an error. As stated above, the error might cause a notification to be sent to a "Fix It" analyst to clean the address in both the sending and receiving systems. Or it might hard-stop the record and the "Fix It" analyst would only need to fix the address in the originating system and push the record through integration again.

I have seen this kind of monitoring be as simple as a spreadsheet from an integration log or as robust as a Web application that allows the business users to watch the data comparisons in real time and may also provide a mechanism to "tickle" or force a record to be sent through integration again once the error is resolved. Either way, it is usually people who need to make the corrections. There are applications that can be programmed to be smart enough to do some error correction on their own. Address standardization is one of the most common use cases for those applications. But the "automatic" correction can be applied to identified data transpositions, i.e. 2103 instead of 2013, and other quantifiable rules.

Data at Rest

Data at Rest is measured by implementing a rules engine that scans the database for anomalies based on business rules. This is the most holistic approach to information quality. In addition to being the most comprehensive in scope, tracking information quality in this manner allows for targeted clean-up. Generally, this trending of data is the metrics your company executives will care about. Is your data getting better or worse now that it is governed? It is an important governance measure.

Measurement and Metrics

It is helpful to know what information is required, important, or just desired in order to prioritize clean-up efforts.

For example, if Gender is an important data element in your business, a rule could be written to report records with no value in the Gender field. Reports should provide counts of records with missing data as well as a count of all records where a gender makes sense (you would not have gender on a hospital, for example). And the reports should include enough specificity for the Data Quality or Fix-It analysts to identify the specific records with errors.

With this set of information, the analyst will understand the numerator (number missing) and the denominator (total number of records with a possible gender field) and can calculate the "health" of that data element as a simple percentage.

This is a method of establishing measurements. Once you can measure the data, you will need to establish a goal or target for the measurement. This is the metric.

Developing reports or dashboards that use the measures and metrics to visualize the health of the data is a powerful tool to prove the success of the governance program.

Information Quality Dimensions

Measuring the quality of your data is best accomplished by establishing a set of Information Quality Dimensions. There are nine dimensions commonly in use across industries. *(Download an editable version at* www.getgoverned.com/9_dimensions*) or see the references section of the book for a handy definition sheet.)*

These may be modified for your specific definitions:

1. **Conformed**: Does it conform to the data standards (i.e. MM/DD/YYYY for date or

###-##-#### for Social Security Number)?

2. **Valid**: Beyond Conformance, does the information make sense. For example: year in a date is within the expected range (2103 vs 2013) or no dummy values such as 999-99-9999 for SSN.

3. **Complete**: No missing values.

4. **Accurate**: Requires an authoritative source to compare against. Sometimes called "correct."

5. **Consistent**: is the information the same between systems/applications.

6. **Unique**: If expected, is the information unique within the data set.

7. **Available**: Is the information accessible and/or was the application running during business hours or according to Service Level Agreements.

8. **Timely**: Was the information entered into the system or application in a manner that complied with turnaround times or SLAs.

9. **Current**: How likely is the information to represent "Now."

Blockers

It is easy to say that you are going to set up a data and information quality program. But there will be things that try to get in the way. The first one will be cost. There is an inherent cost to programming an application to apply system-enforced rules, or to automatically alert when an error is made, or to churn through data in a database to pull out trends of data. Usually this cost is an up-front cost to implement and then a small ongoing cost for technical support and business response and monitoring.

It may be difficult to quantify the monetary value of bad data. Usually it must be shown to impact some kind of transactional process, whether that is from loss of sales or incorrectly paid claims. It is possible to calculate a cost if you can get your leadership to quantify the negative impact of a bad experience by a customer. There are strategies for calculating the value of customer experience.

Another method is to calculate value based on non-quantifiable benefits. These include things such as avoiding bad publicity or protecting the brand (although a mature company will have a calculation for the value of their brand and ways to calculate impacts that hurt it).

Cost-avoidance is another method to calculate benefits. For example, if you had been previously fined for bad data that was exposed to a regulator or customer, avoiding those costs in the future is a good method to show value. It also tends to have an emotional pull since those public embarrassments are things that executives try to avoid.

Setting up a Data and Information Quality program is a simple eight step process. Categorizing, reporting, and managing to metrics are more complicated. The data quality dimensions provide a framework for how to think about information quality. And creating sub-categories of Data on the Move, Data at Rest and Operational data help you define the ways to measure the information quality. And you know how to identify blockers and benefits.

Chapter 7 – Small Business Corner

Setting up a Data Quality program is a fundamental component of any business. Information is money. And "bad" information equates to lost revenue or unnecessary costs. Adopting the nine data quality dimensions is worth the time and effort. And like everything else, if done early, when your company is small, it will become an integral part of your culture and will avoid a costly change management and program implementation cost later.

Developing a system to monitor and ensure that data stays accurate and complete will also benefit your company as it grows.

Chapter 8 – Transfer to Operations

"Think ahead.

Don't let day-to-day operations drive out planning."

Donald Rumsfeld

The program is now established. Your key contributors have been engaged. They know their roles and they know the roadmap. You have a few loose ends to tie up and then you will be ready to support the ongoing governance activities.

Let's revisit your Roadmap. What activities need to continue this year? What are the activities for next year? Most companies begin their project funding and planning in June or July for the following fiscal year (about six months before the end of the current fiscal year). As you have worked through this first year of data governance, you have accomplished a lot of things.

It is likely that you have identified the need for some kind of software solution to support the operating model. Three main areas should be evaluated: end-to-end workflow management tools, data lineage tools, and a Glossary/EIM tool. You may need other tools as well, or you might have one or more of the three critical tools already installed. You may need a dedicated project or two with strategic funding to implement a tool or just to build out the data quality dashboards.

Asking for funding requires that you are able to clearly define the need, the benefits and an estimated cost. It will also require that your IT partners agree that no solution is available. Or if it is available, what it will cost to implement your use case for governance

Beyond tooling, though, the primary need for the operating model is staff. Data Governance should fall under a Chief Data Officer, VP of Analytics and Governance, or some other specific leader who will have the accountability to ensure that data is well stewarded. That leader should actively support and help plan the specific staffing model needed.

The most important role is to have a Vice President or Director of Governance. Since you have been the Driver of the program, it is likely that you will be placed in that role, and if that interests you, it may be an important part of the discussion when you first take on the task of implementing the program. But if it is not you who will be placed in the leadership role, you will have the information to help align on the specific skills and knowledge set needed for the position. They should have experience with a governance organization and have the ability to influence across the organization in a matrixed environment as well as manage a high performing team. Once that leader is chosen, they will need people to do the work.

There are two main schools of thought about a governance organization. The first is that it is staffed primarily by business subject matter experts, usually the data stewards, who have a dotted line accountability to the Governance Officer. This is a model that can work, but especially in a new program, the time demands on these people are a significant strain on their "day jobs."

The other model is to have centralized staff that report to the governance officer. These people, managers or analysts, would be assigned to manage the issues, policies, quality, and other governance activities for a single domain. They would be full time data stewards. They may report to the governance officer with a dotted line accountability to the data owner. Or they may report to the Data Owner with dotted lined authority to the data officer. Either way, one person for each domain will be needed.

These analysts/managers should represent the needs and interests of their domain. They should have an active voice in strategy sessions and should work closely with the people who develop DLP's and business processes for the creators, modifiers and consumers of information. My recommendation is that regardless of reporting structure, they are embedded with the business teams that they represent. This builds a bridge of trust and provides more opportunity to be a subject matter expert in their domain.

Once the data stewards are assigned, there is the matter of the Data Quality analysts and the Fix-It analysts. Both of these groups need to have deep subject matter expertise. They could also report into the governance organization, but since the Fix-It analysts, specifically, will work directly in the User Interface to correct errors, it is a reasonable model to have them report into the business operation with dotted line accountability to the governance officer.

The activities that remain will depend in large amount on the activities that you completed during the kick-off year. Anything that was deferred or placed on the Roadmap for future consideration will need support staff and funds to complete. The main operational activities include data quality clean-up and monitoring, issue resolution and tracking, supporting projects implementing additional tooling, and ensuring that the data steward's concerns and items are socialized and understood across the enterprise.

What may change in the transition to operations is the support structure and committees.

The Steering Committee may roll their responsibilities into some other oversight function. And the data stewards may go back to their regular jobs. Having the people available to pick up all remaining work will be an important part of keeping the program alive, even after the initial milestones are completed.

The leader of the ongoing operations model will need to set specific targets and develop metrics for the governance staff, whether direct report or dotted line. They will need to get the support of the domain owners and steering committee to ensure that the SMEs will still be available. The data quality work will need to be reported at least monthly. A plan should be in place to drive continued improvement. Areas that are not mature will need additional focus. The Enterprise Logical Data Model will need continued work to capture the full end-to-end life-cycle of data. Policy management and approvals will need to have oversight. And the Code Map will need an owner who maintains the Master conform codes and ensures that STTM mapping is aligned to industry standard codes.

The ongoing data strategy work will be a new part of the blueprinting work that most organizations refresh at least annually. It will be very important that the defined strategies are included in the blueprints and goals of the organization. The complex data strategy and inventory documentation will be the foundation of growing and maturing the governance process.

If you have ever done project management, you know that the operational support model is often the most difficult part of a project. There are many tasks to do, such as developing an ongoing communication model, policies, and Desk Level Procedures to govern the work of the team.

All of this, and more, will be the work of the ongoing staff model. If you are lucky and your leadership understands the need for dedicated staff and are willing to fund them, you should take advantage of that quickly. If you are not getting additional staff and they will be sourced from the various business units, make sure that you have met with the direct supervisor and/or the domain owner to ensure support and dedicated time.

Getting approval for the operating model is among the final steps in setting up the program.

Chapter 8 – Small Business Corner

The ideas in this chapter are applicable to small and large companies, alike. Whatever level of governance program you have implemented, it will need nourishment to keep it alive and ensure it remains a vital part of your culture.

Chapter 9 – Conclusion

"There are better starters than me
but I'm a strong finisher."
Usain Bolt

Pull up your checklist. How many of the things you identified as needing to be done are complete? How many do you have left?

Do you remember why you are building a data governance program in the first place?

Remember the story of Mark in the Emergency Room and how his life could have been taken away by something as simple as a missing system enforced rule about medication allergies in the drug ordering system. Remember how satisfying it was to get the right Venti Mocha Frappuccino this morning with your name on the cup. Think about how satisfying it is to call the bank and when you do get to talk to a person they know who you are and can solve your problem.

We all want those kinds of assurances in our daily life. Your company has customers and employees, both of whom deserve that kind of service and satisfaction. Data governance provides the framework to deliver those kinds of positive interactions.

We have covered a lot of information in this book. I hope that it is a handbook that you can use to structure and implement your governance program. I stand ready to help. Visit my website at www.getgoverned.com. You will find resources available for download and special "reader discounts" for personal or group training – enter code "reader" at check-out. If you are still uncomfortable or have some specific trouble spots, my team or I can provide additional training or consultation to help you through any trouble spots or just give you the jumpstart you need to Get Governed!

Resources

Agile Project Management Resources

Of all the project management methodologies, Agile Scrum is my favorite. It has been proven time and again to be the most efficient method, and I am often surprised when Waterfall development is suggested for anything other than most simple of projects. Following is a list of online resources to give you more information:

1. Wikipedia:
   https://en.wikipedia.org/wiki/Agile_software_development
2. The Agile Manifesto:
   http://agilemanifesto.org/history.html
3. Agile Project Management for Dummies:
   http://www.dummies.com/careers/project-management/agile-project-management-for-dummies-cheat-sheet/
4. Thoughtworks- Agile Project Management:
   https://www.thoughtworks.com/agile-project-management
5. Mountain Goat software guide to Scrum:
   https://www.mountaingoatsoftware.com/agile/scrum

White Paper: Common Trouble Spots When Implementing Data Governance

Overview: Data Governance is complicated. Implementing a program for any size organization can create challenges that are new and expose weaknesses in a company's systems or processes. Although these challenges are unique to each company, there are some common themes. Each of these problem areas can be solved either by engaging an outside company to provide expertise or by cultivating that expertise within a few key individuals, which we'll call Mentors, within the organization.

Problem Areas: Several key problem areas may become evident within the first 18 months of implementing a data governance program. These fall under the following topics: Education of the Stewards; Having the Right People in the Right Roles; Roles & Responsibilities; Stakeholder Engagement; and Data Quality. Stewards must also serve in an advisory role and be the point of contact for communications.

Education of the Stewards: The Data Steward role is often new for the company. It is a new way of thinking. It requires looking beyond where we create and manage data and understanding how the data is consumed. End-to-end thinking is surprisingly uncommon in today's environment of specialization. Functions within an organization are often so specialized that the people doing them may have little or no exposure to how their actions affect other areas of the company. The Data Stewards need to be given access and empowerment to look across boundaries to ensure that information is shepherded across systems and teams. Most Stewards will need education on this new perspective as well as some guidance to navigate the waters while learning the skills.

Right People in the Right Roles: Understanding and defining what a Data Steward's role should be is often a struggle. Each of the Data Stewards has a different level of understanding of the organization's leadership model, data, processes, and disciplines needed to support the governance activities across the boundaries of an organization. Stewards who have job titles of Vice President or Director are generally comfortable and familiar with the role of the Steering Committee and how to provide information to that group (although what to report may still be a mystery), but they may be far outside of their comfort level when asked to make decisions about a data model or glossary term. Stewards with the job title of Analyst or Manager may be very comfortable performing the review of Glossary terms, data quality work, or the specifics of how data is managed, but they may not have the background to ensure proper Stakeholder Engagement and Communication is occurring. Stewards of any job title may be unfamiliar with data modeling, information models, and technical integrations.

Data Steward activities are needed in at least three varieties:

1. Strategic direction at the 30,000-foot and above level: These are the Sr. Mangers and above who understand the strategies and initiatives occurring in their operational area. These Stewards can make decisions and give approvals for initiatives and efforts.

2. Hands-on-keyboard-level: These are primarily Analysts, with some Managers, Supervisors and Program Managers mixed in. These Stewards understand the data as it is used and managed at a tactical level. They can make decisions and give approvals at the data element level.

3. Technically savvy business Subject Matter Experts who can interpret and advise on the structures and artifacts, such as data models and Source to Target Documents, ensuring that data becomes usable information and is available when and where it is needed.

Very few organizations set up their program to include all three levels of Data Steward. What this causes is gaps in some business areas or domains that don't have all three levels represented and the opposite problem where too many representatives in an area are named stewards to avoid gaps. Both problems could easily be solved if we identify the right people, create an active engagement model, and apply some project management discipline to the process.

Roles and Responsibilities: The specific tasks that a Steward must perform is often relatively new and unpracticed, and their knowledge is driven, in large part, by the specific involvement with a project. Beyond representation in projects, Data Stewards are accountable for things such as approving changes to the Code Map document, data model changes in the systems that hold their work, population and/or modification of a Data Lineage tool, "tuning" and working tasks in a Master Data Management software in a data warehouse, and resolution of confusion or conflicts about the method of solving for "new" things.

The method of review, documentation of rules, agreements or decisions, and the engagement model with other business unit SME's is often not well defined. Putting in place a model to support the Stewards will make a positive difference in understanding and managing the end-to-end data flows and processes. Having a standard format and location to hold and manage documents will also be a part of defining the roles and responsibilities.

Stakeholder Engagement: Almost always, Data Stewards are expected to represent business units and organizations that are beyond the unit where they perform their "day job." For example, a "Membership" (i.e. client, patient, account holder) Steward may work for the department that enrolls new individual members, but may have little understanding of the work done by the team that enrolls groups. Stewards must engage and inform the stakeholders and SMEs from those adjacent business areas, as appropriate. A solution may be to have a Steward from each group, but that begins to increase the overhead costs, time and complexity.

This illustrates the need for the Data Stewards to have an appropriate communication plan with these stakeholder groups. Many of the groups without a Steward may be completely unaware that the Data Governance organization exists and don't know what decisions may be made on their behalf.

Data Quality: Where, What and How to measure and improve data quality in a Domain is complicated. In addition to the need to cross-over between different business units, just getting access to the data can be challenging. Defining what is important to measure is something the Stewards need to own. Looking at data in new ways and doing so consistently across Domains forces us to challenge our perspective and look up and out with considerations that may be very different from our "day job." Ultimately, the quality of a company's data and consistency of information has a direct impact on the experience of customers and employees and, ultimately, on the bottom line financials. A role of the Data Steward is to help organizations avoid being penny-wise and pound-foolish by looking for synergies and other opportunities to leverage best practices.

Advisory Role: Data Stewards should serve in an advisory capacity on enterprise and strategic initiatives. These items may be Operational in nature and would be appropriately raised and discussed in the Steward Council meetings. Other initiatives are within strategic portfolio and project planning. Initiatives such as the following are good candidates for the Data Stewards to engage around and help coordinate information and decision making:

- Data Marts
- Automation
- End-to-end data flows
- Glossaries and Data Models

Understanding and evaluating the initiatives, providing input on level of effort and level of risk, identifying opportunities for economies of scale, and advising on the "right thing to do" for the Enterprise and Data Domains, not just business units, will help grow the efficiency of operations.

Point of Contact and Communication: Many problems are solved in silos because it is hard to define the right points of contact. The Data Stewards should understand who in their Domain does what and should be able to serve as initial points of contact to triage questions to the correct stakeholder. They should also be communicating general Domain news back to the full complement of the Steward Council as well as the business unit SMEs and stakeholders. This is a critical step that is often overlooked.

Solutions: Whether your organization is facing one, many, or all of these trouble spots, the recommended course of action is to provide mentors to the Stewards. These mentors could be from an outside consulting firm or a selected number of Stewards could be sent for training. Either way, having people with the understanding of the Who, What, Where, and How of Data Governance that can serve as mentors will elevate the experience of the Stewards and greatly improve the outcomes of the program. Further, establishing several Governance Leads to serve as guides toward a functional model and give them some oversight authority of the activities occurring will help fill gaps and enable smoother operations.

Summary: Data Governance is a complex topic and becoming a Data Steward is not an easy thing to do. By understanding the problem areas and putting a support structure in place, you can minimize negative impact on the individual Stewards while improving the overall functionality of the role.

Change Management Refresher

Change defies Gravity. Change goes against the natural tendency of things and people to settle. But change is an important aspect of success in today's business world. The globalization of business requires flexibility and agility as we maneuver and elbow our way into a competitive advantage in a quickly changing environment. The transition of the flow of information from the paper and mail/fax based system of just 15 years ago to a world of social media, instant tweeting and speed-of-light email, video conferencing, and instant messaging requires that companies adopt a change management strategy as both a method to stay competitive and a force to defy gravity.

To help companies better cope with the process of change, I have developed the CHANGE method.

C – Commit to Change

H – Have a Strong Vision

A – Activate your Change Champions

N – New is Always Better – Changing the Culture

G – Generate Excitement (through Short-Term Wins)

E – Empower Employees to Change (Adopt a Culture of Continuous Improvement)

Let's go into a bit more detail on each one.

C – Commit to Change

In order to affect change in your organization, the Leadership Team (preferably the C-suite) must be committed to real and lasting change. Short-term change won't stick and is a waste of everyone's time and money. Make sure you know what Outcomes you are expecting from the change. Be crystal clear about them and that they align with your Strategic Vision.

Commitment means more than writing a blog post or announcing it at a Town Hall or Leadership meeting. Commitment means that it guides your decisions and is part of your communications to convince your employees that you mean it and that you are willing to model the change. You should expect to go through the same Change Continuum as your employees. But you should commit to go through it first so that you can guide them.

What is the Change Continuum? It is the path that everyone must traverse before truly accepting change. Look at the following graphic. Study it. Do you recognize these feelings, words and actions in yourself? Good! That means you are ready to help your employees by Empathizing with what they are going through.

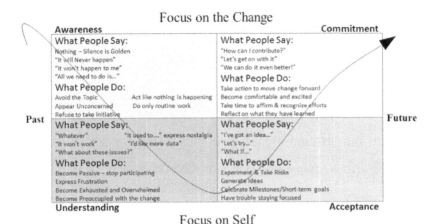

Focus on the Change

Awareness	Commitment
What People Say:	**What People Say:**
Nothing – Silence is Golden	"How can I contribute?"
"It Will Never happen"	"Let's get on with it"
"It won't happen to me"	"We can do it even better!"
"All we need to do is..."	**What People Do:**
What People Do:	Take action to move change forward
Avoid the Topic Act like nothing is happening	Become comfortable and excited
Appear Unconcerned Do only routine work	Take time to affirm & recognize efforts
Refuse to take initiative	Reflect on what they have learned
What People Say:	**What People Say:**
"Whatever" "It used to...." express nostalgia	"I've got an idea..."
"It won't work" "I'd like more data"	"Let's try..."
"What about these issues?"	"What If..."
What People Do:	**What People Do:**
Become Passive – stop participating	Experiment & Take Risks
Express Frustration	Generate Ideas
Become Exhausted and Overwhelmed	Celebrate Milestones/Short-term goals
Become Preoccupied with the change	Have trouble staying focused
Understanding	Acceptance

Past — Future

Focus on Self

The curved line shows the path that we all traverse. We all begin with a budding Awareness of the change but are still focusing on the past. We then begin to have an Understanding of the change. But this brings out our feelings of defensiveness as we focus on how the change will affect "me!" Notice the behaviors and words in this quadrant. If you don't commit to the change before you get here, this might stop you. As a leader, you need to push yourself forward into Acceptance. After all, you committed to the change because you understand the outcomes. It should be easier for you to get through these feelings and steps. Finally, you reach Commitment. This is where you thought you would start. But you're human, too. You will also have to traverse the Change Continuum.

Each of your leaders and employees will traverse the Continuum at their own pace. The next steps will help the organization have a more successful change.

H – Have a Strong Vision

In his ground-breaking book, "Leading Change," John Kotter describes vision as having six characteristics. A good vision is:

1. Imaginable
2. Desirable
3. Feasible
4. Focused
5. Flexible, and
6. Communicable

A clear Vision serves three purposes. First, it clarifies the direction for change, second it motivates people to take action in the right direction, and third, it coordinates the actions of different people or groups.

A Vision statement should be communicable in 60 seconds or less. Think of the "Elevator Speech" concept. Your Vision must be easy enough to express that anyone can memorize the content and repeat it whenever the Commitment starts to waver.

A – Activate your Change Champions (include authority and accountability)

You need a team of people who will be given both the Authority and the Accountability to ensure that the change is implemented according to plan. These are your Change Champions. Think of these people as your Super Heroes! They will literally fight gravity, or the tendency of all people and things to remain in place. They will need the authority to bust through obstacles and move those mossy-stone blockers of change. They will need your 100% support as the blockers "escalate" to try to stop the change. Give your Champions firm direction and complete commitment and they will literally move mountains to accomplish the change.

"Wonder Twin Powers – Activate!" Give your Change Champions a community to support each other. There is strength in numbers. Support builds Resiliency, and that is a critical component to have the fortitude to continue when times get tough – and they will!

The Champions will need to have the Accountability to enact the change. In addition to your support with the correct level of authority, the Change Champions will need to be held accountable. Make sure that this effort is part of their "day-job" with goals and milestones that they are held accountable to for their performance evaluation. Change is extremely hard. If there is an incentive, such as a Bonus or a Raise, for successfully implementing change, your Champions will be far more likely to brave out of their comfort zone and know that you "Have Their Back."

N – New is Always Better – Changing the Culture

Every company has a corporate culture. In almost every case, these have grown up over years, or decades, and are the way things get done. Sayings like "We need to Blue Shield-ize everything" or "This is the Coventry Way" contain within them a tacit acceptance of the status quo. Don't mistake this as the necessary and important work of protecting the Brand. Just like the Vision, the Brand must be protected. But the culture of doing things according to the status quo will be the most difficult thing to overcome.

A very real fear that is likely to come to pass during any change of significance is a journey to the "Valley of Despair." This describes the dip in productivity that occurs as a new system is implemented or even a new business process.

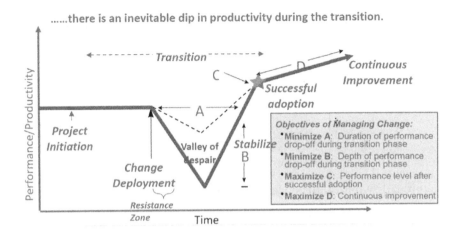

People are naturally inclined to avoid this dip in productivity. You, as a leader, need to give them permission to traverse the frightening loss of productivity. In point of fact, there is a direct correlation between the level of acceptance by leadership, and the expectation that this will occur, and the Duration and Depth of the Valley. In other words, if the Leadership gives their teams "permission" to have a dip in productivity as they go through change, the employees will go through the Valley more quickly with less loss of productivity. When a leader expects change to occur without a dip in productivity, the fear in their employees will actually cause a deeper dive into the Valley and productivity will be lower and last longer than expected.

Before you have that freak-out moment, take a short pause. Pull out your cell phone. Is it the latest smart-phone model? Or have you been content to keep the same old flip-phone you've carried for ten years because it is so reliable. For almost everyone,

209

you will have to agree that New is Always Better. Now breathe, and recognize that these emotions and this process is normal, it's part of change, and 'this too shall pass.'

I once led a program that transitioned a department's work from five systems of record to one single system with integrations to three down-stream systems. It was a series of very significant changes and the management and supervisors went through the change continuum just a few weeks ahead of the need to lead their teams of employees through the changes. The productivity loss in the Valley of Despair continued to drop throughout the 13-month implementation with no prediction of when the drop was going to end and change direction. But on the day the final integration went into production, there was a noticeable shift toward more productivity. Within one month, it was apparent by all metrics that the climb was underway. And the 13-month slide into the Valley reversed in only 3-months. The team was back to pre-implementation volumes. It took another six months to get the backlogged inventory to "normal" levels. But productivity has continued to rise ever since.

G – Generate Excitement (through Short-Term Wins)

Generating Excitement and keeping the teams engaged is an absolutely critical imperative for the Change Champions, Senior Leaders, and front-line managers and supervisors. Celebrating Milestones along the way is a great way to show that the effort to change is understood and appreciated. To borrow from John Kotter's "Leading Change" again, good short-term wins are 1) visible, 2) unambiguous, and 3) Clearly related to the change effort.

The very important role of short term wins is that they:

1. Provide evidence that sacrifices are worth it.
2. Reward change agents with a pat on the back which increases morale and motivation.
3. Helps fine-tune vision and strategies.
4. Overcome critics and self-serving detractors – clear improvement in performance make it difficult for people to block needed change.
5. Keep bosses (Senior Leaders and direct People Leaders) on board with the change.
6. Builds momentum and turns neutrals into supporters.

Celebrations don't have to be extravagant. And, in fact, they shouldn't be. They should be equal to the amount of change. A small milestone may be celebrated by a congratulatory email from the Vice President of the division. A larger milestone or accomplishment may warrant buying pizza for the team. When the goal is achieved, public recognition, monetary rewards, and a special memento (mug, backpack, or other Branded item) should be presented to the Change Champions AND the team that went through the change. Of course, size and amount are dictated by contribution, but don't let the opportunity to reward and recognize your team's accomplishment go unused. People need to know that they are supporting the mission of the company and that they can and do make a difference.

It is important, however, to keep the celebrations in line with the achievement. Rewards and celebrations that occur too frequently or are too large can create a feeling of complacency and minimize the sense of urgency to change. People often mistake reward for acknowledgement of completion. It's important to keep the team motivated and focused on the remaining work while acknowledging the accomplishments.

E – Empower Employees to Change (Adopt a Culture of Continuous Improvement)

When employees are actively engaged in making a difference it is easier to motivate them to change the culture to one of Continuous Improvement. Employees need to know that they are empowered to speak up when they see a possible improvement to a process or the elimination of waste. A company can go out of business because they are "nickel and dimed" to death. Tiny, sometimes imperceptible, amounts of waste add up to big losses. And, I have to admit that when a team has bonded through overcoming the Valley of Despair, they are hungry for more of that feeling of accomplishment. It is a prime opportunity to put mechanisms in place to allow for the continuous improvement of every process.

212

Empower employees to make decisions that affect their own jobs and especially when they improve the experience for the customer. Develop a mindset of Change and an expectation within the culture that finding, reporting, and solving inefficiencies in every process is what gets rewarded through promotions and pay. Incorporate continuous improvement in job descriptions and career ladders. This is how you affect permanent change.

Conclusion: This paper was intended to be only a short refresher on change management. Use the CHANGE method to manage through change: Commit to Change; Have a Strong Vision; Activate Your Champions; New is Always Better – Changing the Culture; Generate Excitement (Through Short-term Wins), and Empower Employees to Change (Adopt a Culture of Continuous Improvement). Take these six steps to heart and affect the CHANGE you want to see in your organization.

Nine Dimensions of Information Quality

1. **Conformed**: Does information conform to the data standards (i.e. MM/DD/YYYY for date or ###-##-#### for Social Security Number).

2. **Valid**: Beyond Conformance, does the information make sense. For example: year in a date is within the expected range (2103 vs 2013) or no dummy values such as 999-99-9999 for SSN.

3. **Complete**: No missing values.

4. **Accurate**: Requires an authoritative source to compare against. Sometimes called "correct."

5. **Consistent**: The information is the same between systems/applications.

6. **Unique**: If expected, the information is unique within the data set.

7. **Available**: The information is accessible and/or the application was running during business hours or according to Service Level Agreements.

8. **Timely**: The information was entered into the system or application in a manner that complied with turnaround times or SLAs.

9. **Current**: How likely is the information to represent "Now?"

Case Study: Information Lifecycle and Interoperability

Abstract: Using health care provider data flowing into a claims management system, this study presents an example of loss of critical information in the exchange from system to system because of lack of governed rules and clear understanding of the lifecycle of information. It demonstrates a need for a holistic view of the flow of information and how governing data can ensure that information is available when and where it is needed. It ties the flow of information to the cost of healthcare and helps illustrate the value of data governance to the mission to lower the costs for all Americans.

Introduction: Interoperability is the ability for systems to exchange and make use of information or groups to work in conjunction with each other.

The Health Information Management Systems Society (HIMMS) describes it as follows: "Interoperability describes the extent to which systems and devices can exchange data, and interpret that shared data. For two systems to be interoperable, they must be able to exchange data and subsequently present that data such that it can be understood by a user.[1]"

Case Presentation: The cost of healthcare insurance premiums is based on the work of actuaries. These financial data scientists mine for claim and outcome information and set the price of healthcare insurance premiums. The goal is to set the price at a level that ensures solvency to cover the predicted future costs of patient claims. They must also minimize risk to the health insurance company of selling Products (health insurance plans we buy) that do not provide sufficient income to meet the financial obligation of the health insurance company. Most health plans are also very concerned about the skyrocketing cost of healthcare and are scouring data for ways to help reduce the costs such that premiums can lower rather than rise so that Americans can afford to pay their insurance premiums.

Interoperability is the ability for information to be understood by two parties, be they systems or people, and made use of to act in concert. Without interoperability data must be manually interpreted and passed along. This opens the very real probability of some loss of content. This loss may be incidental at the point of interpretation, but may in fact be critical several steps down the lifecycle of a process. In the case of healthcare provider information at a health plan, information is managed in a provider data management (PDM) system. The PDM holds demographic information, network participation, location information, quality scores, billing/payment information and pricing pointers related directly to the contractual rates, credentialing and enrollment of the provider as "participating."

In order to pay a claim submitted by a provider, only a small amount of that information is needed – typically: name, Tax ID, location, network, pricing, and payment information. If the system integration between the PDM and the claims processing system only passes the information to pay a claim to a provider, the amount of information exchanged is kept to a minimum. However, the life-cycle of the information does not stop at claims payment.

After a claim is paid to a provider, the information about that claim is passed to a clinical evaluation team with the responsibility to evaluate the care provided, ensure that billing matches acceptable care standards for the diagnosis, and that the physician is qualified and trained appropriately for the scope of practice represented within the billing codes. In order to do those functions, the clinical evaluation team needs information such as the physician's training program, board certification, contractual rates, and aggregated claims data. The clinical evaluation team's system could directly extract information from both the PDM and the claims payment system. But it is much more efficient for this information to aggregate and stay together through the life-cycle rather than requiring "matching logic" to connect PDM provider information with the information and records in the clinical evaluation software.

Beyond clinical evaluation, a health plan employs Medical Informaticists to mine data for clinical trends, population health, and many more things. While they often connect to data lakes and data marts to mine for data to perform advanced analytics, enough information is needed when their business process begins for them to be able to find the information that is relevant.

One step beyond Medical Informatics is Actuarial, which is the group of financial data scientists who evaluate claims and population trends and set pricing for our health care premiums in order to cover the risk to the health plan and provide information to define and price health care Products to employer groups or individuals.

Each of these functions require that the information entered in the PDM be carried along, aggregated with claim, treatment and financial information, and be understandable and usable by each of the teams in the life-cycle of the data.

Outcome: Without appropriate governance ensuring that information retains unique characteristics and markers, the conclusions that shape both the expectations of clinical outcomes and the price of health insurance premiums will be at risk to miss clinical trends that may need intervention or to price a Product too high or too low in the market.

Summary: The enforcement of data standards, clear and understandable transformations and aggregation of data from system to system has a dramatic impact on the lives of all Americans. Clear and accurate information is a necessary part of understanding how healthcare can become more affordable. Data governance is a crucial part of that promise.

References:

[1]http://www.himss.org/library/interoperability-standards/what-is-interoperability

Glossary

Note: Glossary indexed page numbers are based on a 6" x 9" print book. They will most likely not align to the page numbers in electronic copies.

Term	Definition	Pages
Access	Available. When combined with "Security" it generally denotes a user profile or security function that allows the user to view or modify data.	10, 11, 12, 16, 40, 134, 135, 196, 199
Action Item	As part of a project or RAID document, it is a documented assignment with a named owner that is accountable for completion.	71, 72
Advanced Analytics	The science of mining for and extracting information from many data sources for the purpose of explaining or predicting trends and/or behaviors. Common practitioners are Data Scientists or Medical Informaticists.	8, 220
Architect, Architecture	Individual or team who designs systems or solutions.	62, 69, 105, 125, 131, 132, 133, 149, 159, 167
Attribute	Item or entry in a table; used to describe or add additional value to a definition.	xvii, 103, 104, 108, 110, 111, 162

Term	Definition	Pages
Back-end Access	Interfacing with a database directly within the tables, bypassing the User Interface. Usually this is the preferred method of interaction for data analysts and scientists because large amounts of data can be accessed without looking up records individually.	226, 241
Backlog	The collection of user stories needed to complete an Agile project.	31
Big Data	Usually referring to a large data warehouse. This has its own vocabulary sub-set. (see also: *Cloud, Data Lake, Data Warehouse*)	v, 9, 10, 133, 155
Business Process Model	A visual representation of the steps taken to accomplish a task within a defined workflow.	112, 113, 114, 116, 117, 151, 165, 166
Cloud	Information held "off-premise" or "hosted" by a service provider sometimes referred to as a "virtual data lake."	9, 155
CMS	Center for Medicare/Medicaid Services; Part of the department of Health and Human Services.	37, 40
Code Map	A master cross reference document aligning terms,	6, 13, 14, 15, 100, 106, 107, 118, 149, 151,

Term	Definition	Pages
	definitions and *codes* used in various system and business documents to a standard set of values or Conform Codes.	152, 153, 154, 159, 164, 168, 186, 198
Codes	A numerical representation in a data model or system of a business term.	14, 25, 107, 118, 151, 152, 153, 154, 162, 186, 219
Control Chart	A graph that shows how data or a process changes over time.	35, 87
Council	Referring to Data Steward Council.	62, 63, 141, 142, 143, 144, 146, 147, 148, 149, 200, 201
C-Suite	Corporate Leadership, usually comprised of at least a Chief Executive Officer (CEO), Chief Financial Officer (CFO), and Chief Operating Officer (COO). May also include Chief Information Officer (CIO), Chief Technical Officer (CTO), Chief Personnel Officer (CPO), Chief Human Resources Officer (CHRO), Chief Medical Director/Officer (CMD/CMO), Chief Data Officer (CDO), Data Privacy Officer (DPO) or other "Chief Officer" roles.	23, 127, 204
Data	Information in electronic or paper form.	This term is used throughout the

225

Term	Definition	Pages
		book and will not be indexed each time
Data Assets	The collection of data or information that provides the company with the ability to differentiate themselves in the market by leveraging the data available within their own systems, often employing Advanced Analytics. Data Assets can be quantified and, in large corporate organizations, are often part of the financial ledger of company assets.	v, 8, 133, 151, 164
Data Asset Management	The discipline of controlling data or information used by the company.	61, 151, 164, 167
Data Custodian	Usually an Information Technologist who is accountable for the integrity of a system that holds data or information.	8, 126, 130, 131, 132, 142, 149, 164, 167
Data Governance	The activity of defining and organizing structure around information.	This term is used throughout the book and will not be indexed each time
Data Lake	A collection of structured and unstructured data.	9, 133, 144, 145, 155, 220

Term	Definition	Pages
Data Lineage	A systematic way to classify data making it traceable through its life-cycle. This generally includes the metadata of where the information was created, managed, transferred, transformed, merged, consumed, etc.	9, 33, 133, 134, 135, 147, 155, 156, 157, 158, 159, 164, 182, 198
Data Modeler	An individual who creates visual representations of database tables, information systems, or other models of how information interacts, is stored, or held within a computer database or system.	132, 133, 149
Data Owner	Usually the individual in an organization that has the accountability for a domain of data.	7, 128, 129, 130, 132, 142, 147, 148, 184
Data Quality, DQ, and Information Quality	Concerned with the level of accuracy and correctness of the data being governed; may also include any or all of the nine Data Quality Dimensions.	xxi, xxii, 8, 9, 10, 11, 18, 19, 20, 41, 42, 45, 61, 87, 130, 131, 135, 138, 146, 147, 163, 167, 169, 170, 174, 175, 176, 178, 179, 180, 182, 185, 186, 191, 195, 196, 199, 215
Data Quality Analyst	An individual with the responsibility to ensure that information meets the requisite quality standards.	130, 150, 185

Term	Definition	Pages
Data Standards	The agreed upon structure of data or data artifacts that is considered the "correct" state. The standards may be internal standards or may align to an industry standard, such as the International Organization for Standardization (ISO).	10, 61, 176, 215, 221
Data Steward	An individual that has been designated to care for a set of data or data processes who is accountable to the Data Owner for the proper management and care of the data.	7, 62, 70, 75, 76, 121, 122, 125, 126, 127, 128, 129, 130, 132, 138, 141, 142, 143, 144, 145, 146, 147, 148, 149, 150, 164, 167, 168, 183, 184, 185, 186, 195, 196, 197, 198, 199, 200, 201
Data Warehouse	A structured collection of data.	9, 19, 133, 198
Decision	An agreement or consensus on a key component of any undertaking. When part of a RAID document, a Decision serves as justification for the direction of the project.	v, 15, 62, 63, 71, 72, 77, 101, 113, 117, 121, 122, 123, 126, 132, 138, 144, 146, 149, 151, 196, 197, 198, 199, 200, 204, 213
Denormalized Data	Unstructured Data.	162
Desk Level Procedure or DLP	A document that describes the method to maintain information	94, 97, 98, 99, 135, 184, 187

Term	Definition	Pages
	in a system or process.	
DMAIC	An acronym which stands for Define, Measure, Analyze, Improve and Control; A Six Sigma methodology for improving data or processes.	35, 169
Document Management	A method of managing written materials in a manner that is consistent and accessible. It includes Policies about documents, security and access, filing systems and retention.	xxi, 10
Domain	A set of data that is related by topic. For example, a Financial Domain would be the data and information that is related to money, income, and/or accounting. A Customer Domain would be the data and information that relates to the customer including demographic data, purchasing habits, etc.	7, 61, 68, 69, 75, 76, 128, 138, 139, 141, 145, 147, 156, 162, 164, 184, 186, 188, 198, 199, 200, 201
Driver	The person accountable to push a project or initiative forward. In projects, the Driver is usually accountable to the Owner. Project Managers are expected to follow the direction	48, 60, 64, 65, 75, 76, 127, 183

Term	Definition	Pages
	of the Driver.	
Enterprise Data Governance or EDG	The structure of organization across a company, or enterprise, intended to manage and control the company's data assets and practices.	8, 103
Enterprise Information Model or EIM	Visual representation of the structure, systems, infrastructure and definitions that make up the flow of information across an enterprise.	108, 111, 112, 119, 165, 182
Enterprise Logical Data Model or ELDM	The visual representation of business data and concepts modeled into relational structures that are reflective of system physical models but expressed in business terms.	108, 111, 119, 164, 165, 167, 186
ETL or ELT	Extract/Transform/ Load or Extract/Load/ Transform is a method of moving information from one system (Extract), changing the structure, codes, or rules around the data (Transform) and inserting into the receiving system (Load). The decision to use ETL or ELT is sometimes dictated by system components, preference of the development team, or	173

Term	Definition	Pages
	other data considerations.	
Executive Steering Committee or Steering Committee	The group of leaders who direct governance activities.	62, 63, 69, 71, 125, 126, 127, 128, 130, 132, 138, 139, 143, 147, 148, 167, 186, 196
Fish Bone Diagram	The visualization of information to identify potential cause and effect for root cause analysis. Also called an Ishikawa diagram after the inventor of the chart.	35
Fix-It Analyst	Similar to a Data Quality Analyst, the individual who will made changes or modification of information when a quality error or deviation is identified.	130, 131, 150, 175, 185
Information Journey Method	A six-step method of organizing information to support information seeking, information judgments, information use and information sharing. The six steps are as follows. 1. Determine the need for information or Topic Introduction. 2. Topic-oriented information gathering - seeking information. 3. Judgement and evaluation or exploration of obtained	20

231

Term	Definition	Pages
	information. 4. Making sense of information. 5. Identifying any Gaps in the information (if found, return to step 2). 6. Ingesting information to enable learning, problem solving, or sharing.	
Information Lifecycle	The end-to-end journey of information from where it is originally created or managed through various transformations to use by the consumers of the information.	12, 191, 217
Information Waste	Duplicative or proprietary data that adds confusion or does not add value to a process. Information Waste adds cost without adding value.	7, 15
Integration	The process of transferring information from one system to another.	10, 13, 107, 112, 114, 115, 116, 133, 154, 158, 161, 173, 174, 197, 210, 219
Interoperability	The idea of connecting two or more systems or business processes into a single, cohesive function. Interoperability applies to systems and business units within a single company as well	10, 14, 15, 107, 155, 168, 191, 217, 218

Term	Definition	Pages
	as when data or processes must be shared with an outside entity as allowed by contractual agreement. The key to interoperability is the need for all parties involved to operate with consistent terminology, code sets and data structures.	
International Organization for Standardization or ISO	A neutral organization that creates data sets to be used by parties throughout the world to bring uniformity and allow for interoperability.	14, 107, 152, 153
Ishikawa	The inventor of the Fish Bone diagram used for Cause and Effect Analysis and Root Cause Analysis.	35
Issue	An Issue is something that is currently blocking the progress of a project. A mitigation plan must be put into place before the project can move forward in one or more areas.	49, 52, 67, 71, 72, 83, 84, 86, 87, 131, 146, 164, 184, 185
Lean	A Process Improvement methodology that seeks to remove waste from a process.	34, 35, 36, 42

Term	Definition	Pages
Master Data Management or MDM	A method of using algorithms and rules to match and merge information into a "Golden Record." The outcome of an MDM system is intended to be a single record with all of the relevant "truth" about that entity/record, regardless of the number of instances or systems that must be combined to get to that single record.	10, 135, 198
Master Definitions	The set of definitions approved as the "truth" for your organization or industry. System or business unit specific definitions should be mapped to an agreed upon master set, usually found in a glossary.	14
Matrixed Organization or Matrixed Environment	An accountability structure wherein parties do not have direct employment oversight of resources but must use influence to achieve cooperation.	127, 128, 183
Metadata	Information about data. For example, #hashtags on Twitter, which help the application sort and deliver content, or counts of the number of cups of coffee sold at a diner between	9, 10, 27, 45, 166

Term	Definition	Pages
	eight and nine in the morning.	
NCQA	National Committee for Quality Assurance. A common accreditation body for health insurance plans.	37
Normalized Data	Terminology used to describe a state of information in a database that has been optimized to reduce redundancy or extra processing time by a system.	162
Off-Prem, Off-Premise, or Hosted	Installed/held in a location of a service provider and available via an internet link.	9, 10
Offshore	Terminology used to indicate that the workforce is located outside of the country of the main company headquarters. Often used by North American countries to refer to work and workers outsourced to other countries.	12
On-Prem, On-Premise	Installed/held on the premise or property of the company.	10
Onshore	Terminology used to indicate that the workforce is located within the same country as the main company headquarters.	12

Term	Definition	Pages
Operating Model, Operational	A term used to describe the people, processes and technology that combine to provide structure to an operation.	xviii, 21, 40, 52, 53, 69, 70, 71, 72, 116, 124, 137, 171, 172, 179, 182, 185, 187, 188, 197, 200
Pareto Chart	A type of chart that contains both bars and a line graph, where individual values are represented in descending order by bars, and the cumulative total is represented by the ascending line.	36, 88
Parking Lot	A term used in planning or design sessions to identify topics or tasks that do not align to the current topic but are important to some member of the group. The "parking lot" allows the facilitator to write down the topic to be revisited later. Thus, acknowledging the input, but not letting the conversation be pulled off-topic.	51, 69, 71
Phase Gate	A formal review process of a project at which time the project Owner and/or Driver approves the deliverables and allows the project to move to the next segment of work.	30, 31, 33, 51, 71

Term	Definition	Pages
PHI	Personal Health Information	41
PII	Personally Identifying Information	41
Policy or Policies	A rule or set of rules that define what is acceptable or expected.	xxii, 6, 7, 10, 11, 12, 24, 28, 29, 33, 37, 42, 45, 61, 63, 77, 78, 79, 82, 94, 95, 96, 97, 98, 99, 100, 118, 129, 130, 138, 142, 144, 150, 164, 167, 184, 186, 187
Privacy	Regulations governing the appropriate use of information and the requirement that some information be maintained in a Private manner. It implies that dictated standards are followed.	41, 141
RAID	RAID is an abbreviation for Risks, Action Items, Issues, Decisions. It is used in project management to track and manage important components hampering or supporting success.	71
Reference Data or Reference Values	Lists of acceptable "answers" that feed drop-down lists in the User Interface of a system. Examples are lists of States or Countries.	106, 118, 150, 156

Term	Definition	Pages
Risk	An item that has a likely chance of occurring that may hinder success. Documenting Risks helps you plan how to avoid them. Every identified Risk requires a Mitigation Plan to avoid or recover from the Risk.	61, 71, 72, 83, 84, 85, 86, 200, 218, 220
Roadmap	A document or set of documents that outlines the path to achieve a strategic initiative or goal.	16, 51, 52, 69, 71, 72, 117, 181, 185
Root Cause Analysis	A method of investigation or problems solving that drills down through steps of a process to find the cause (or root) of the problem.	14, 131, 135, 150, 164
Scatter Plot Diagrams	A graphic representation of two or more variables that visually help identify correlation.	88
Security	The process of protecting information through protocols that limit access to systems or data. Passwords, user profiles, and encryption of data all fall under this heading.	10, 11, 12, 26, 28, 133, 135, 142
Six Sigma	A management technique used to improve a set of processes by defining "optimal state" and	34, 35, 87, 88, 150, 169

Term	Definition	Pages
	measuring deviations from that state.	
Sprint	A time period in an Agile project, usually 2-weeks. All phases of Planning, Design, Development, and Unit/QA/UAT testing are completed for one or more User Stories (outcomes) per sprint.	30, 31, 32
SQL - Structured Query Language	Usually pronounced "see quell" it is used to communicate with or query a database. According to ANSI (American National Standards Institute), it is the standard language for relational database management systems.	13, 150
Stakeholder	A party who has an interest in or is affected by an activity or change.	v, vi, 46, 50, 51, 54, 55, 57, 58, 59, 60, 62, 65, 66, 67, 70, 72, 74, 82, 86, 129, 130, 142, 159, 195, 196, 199, 201
Standard Deviation	A measure that is used to quantify the amount of variation from the accepted normal value.	34 – 35
Steering Committee or Executive Steering Committee	The group of leaders who direct activities.	62, 63, 69, 71, 125, 126, 127, 128, 130, 132, 138, 139, 143, 147, 148, 167, 186, 196

Term	Definition	Pages
Steward Council	The governing organization of the Data Stewards.	142, 146, 148, 149, 200, 201
Structured Data	Usually referring to data in a relational database.	6, 25, 145, 162, 163, 164
STTM - Source To Target Map	A document that describes the way data is transformed during the ETL or ELT of an integration. It can indicate instructions as simple as "direct move," define standard default values for dates or blanks fields, and/or include complicated rules for the transformation from one system to the next.	13, 186
Swim Lane	A box that contains the steps taken by a specific group, person or business unit when describing an end-to-end process.	113
Transformation	Change or modification. The modification of data found in one system to fit into the structures and/or rules of another systems. Generally considered to be part of an ETL process.	xviii, xix, 10, 12, 13, 14, 25, 133, 135, 155, 158, 221
Unstructured Data	Usually referring to data in business applications such as Word, Excel, Access,	7, 9, 145, 161, 162, 163, 164

Term	Definition	Pages
	picture libraries, etc.	
URAC	Utilization Review Accreditation Commission – an accrediting body for health care organizations.	37
User Interface	The part of an Application, Program or System that is accessible as the method to interact with the program. This is usually considered "front-end" access (as opposed to interacting with the back-end database tables).	106, 150, 164, 185
User Story	A Requirement in an Agile project. A user story identifies who needs the requirement, what expected outcome they want from the work, the reason they need the outcome, and a clear statement of what "done" means. It is usually structured using this set of phrases: As a <insert title>, I need the system to <verb> <a thing>, So that I can <Outcome Statement>. I will know when I am done when <specific success criteria>. For Example, "As a Reporting Analyst, I need the	31, 78, 80

Term	Definition	Pages
	system to make Addresses available, so that I can deliver mailing lists to the communications team. I will know I am done when I have properly formatted addresses that conform to USPS standards which can be extracted from the database using SQL statements."	
Value Stream Map	Process flow diagram that identifies the steps in a process that add financial value.	99

Acknowledgments

My life has been a series of learning events. Never easy, but I'm not an easy person. I believe in challenging myself and everyone around me until we get to a moment of brilliant breakthrough. There is always something better that I can become; always something better that we can become together.

I suppose I have my father, Birdell Sorensen, to thank. He was a man of that Greatest Generation - born in 1921, veteran of WW II, quiet, humble, thirsty for knowledge, born with a wanderer's soul and confined to bed by Multiple Sclerosis. I'm a caboose of a brood of nine. My mom worked; my dad raised me. He needed me to challenge him to get up every morning and not give up. He needed me to be independent, from almost the moment I could walk. And so I was. And so I am.

School, and then work, were always easy regardless of topic or field. I'm a quick learner. And my dad and I had read the entire encyclopedia and dictionary a couple of times before I got to middle school. He built the connections of the ultimate generalist with big picture thinking and an understanding of how every decision, every action will have a consequence, for someone, somewhere.

The hardest lesson, humility, is one I learned through my first marriage. I could not control his choices or his actions. I learned that I could only control my own actions and improve myself. I read many of the great self-help books and found that even in duty, there is a quiet dignity.

And through him, I became a mother of four amazing and diverse children. Pick the four points on a compass and each is heading in a different direction with different beliefs and desires. For Subrina, Autumn, Dale and Robert, I am grateful. I love each one of you more than I once thought it was possible to love. I learned through the act and choice of motherhood to have the greatest humility. But I persisted, because they counted on me. The first thing I ever did that was hard, maybe too hard.

There was a moment, unexpected and unexplained, when everything turned full circle and I experience true and pure love. I met Stephen. From that moment until today the adventure, fun, and simple joy to be alive has continued to grow until they fill me and the entire universe with hope, strength, and love.

And then we found others; friends that had always been in our souls, but not yet in our lives. And our love and joy multiplied exponentially until there isn't anyone, anywhere that is outside of its boundaries. I must mention a few people specifically, but there are so many that I will never manage them all: Todd and Lori Grimmett, Edie and Ken Lamphere, John and Nikki Hunter, Dave and Annette Mitchell, Andreas and Shadi Amundin, Wendy and Brian Johnson, Jason and Caryn Hagen, John Fernandez and Cara Minear and our beautiful Goddaughter, Gravity. You bring balance, harmony, wisdom, challenge, and excellence to our life!

Finally, I acknowledge you, the reader. Thank you for trusting me to teach the things I have learned from two degrees, 30+ years in business and a thousand white papers, books, and conversations with architects, data modelers, business analysts, data scientists, business leaders, friends, and of course, Stephen. I hope we get to spend more time together!

About the Author

Morgan Templar has always been fascinated by the way things work. From electronics to musical instruments, the inner workings of the human mind and the massive public relations/social media movements in society, she is entranced by the similarities, patterns, and rhythms that cross topic and boundaries. She describes herself as a specialist at being a generalist.

Morgan has worked in finance, technology and healthcare. She has held many titles and excelled at many things, but always seems to find a way to focus on rules, structures, and efficiency. Governance, quality, continuous improvement and process efficiency are music to her ears and are the hum of a well-oiled machine.

Morgan is the Chief Executive Officer at Sierra Innovation Solutions. She provides consultation services to solve governance, quality and data issues and regularly speaks at conferences on a variety of business topics. She has a Master of Science in Health Administration from The Ohio University and a Bachelor of Science in Public Relations from the University of Utah.

Morgan lives with her husband, Stephen, in Rescue, CA on thirteen acres of holly, chestnut and oak forest with a view of the mountains surrounding Lake Tahoe.

Website: www.getgoverned.com

Email: morgan@getgoverned.com

Facebook:
https://www.facebook.com/theauthormorgantemplar/

LinkedIn: https://www.linkedin.com/in/morgantemplar

Thank You

First, I must thank my mentor and friend, Nanci Ziegler. For providing a stage and a platform from which to evangelize my message. And for her prodding and support, without which I would never have written this book.

Thanks to Edie Parker-Lamphere, for head-hunting me to California and giving me the support and encouragement of an amazing boss and the love of a best friend.

Thanks to Andreas Amundin, for inventing PrimaryScape™ notation. And for being my friend and collaborator during an incredibly productive and creative 14-month period.

Appreciation goes to my children, friends and family who gave me the space and time to create while knowing that I would come out the other side loving you even more. Thanks for the puppy time when I needed it, and for understanding when I couldn't come up for air.

Thank you to my dear friends and fellow authors in the Chrysalis Mastermind. I love each of you and appreciate your guidance, editing, and influence on the contents and structure of this book.

My deep appreciation goes to my creative team, editors, artists, advanced readers, and book launch team. Your enthusiasm and support has brought this book forth and allowed me the space to be excited about data and governance!